Selling with T.R.U.S.T.®

How to Create Extraordinary Sales Success as an In-Home Sales Professional

By Tom Piscitelli

and John Sedgwick

Selling with T.R.U.S.

How to Create Extraordinary Sales Success as an In-Home Sales Professional

Published by:

Tom Piscitelli
2146 NW Boulder Way Drive
Issaquah, WA 98027
www.sellingTRUST.com

Cover Designed by:

Megan LaSalla
www.mhldesigns.com

Printed by: Lightning Source Inc.
ISBN-13: 9780615320809
Printed in the United States of America

Acknowledgements:

I'd like to particularly acknowledge my long time friend, business associate, mentor and coach John Sedgwick who was the driving force in getting this book out of our heads and onto paper.

Lonna Hanson formatted the book, did the final proofreading, and assisted with printing. Megan LaSalla designed the cover and helped us through the final stages of the printing process. Carol LaCroix provided many suggestions for improvements. Robin Mitchell was the first to read the manuscript and her enthusiastic support was appreciated. Mark Matteson proffered his usual valuable advice. Honeywell, Inc. gave me the way to leap from two decades of working in business to full time training and consulting.

This book is dedicated to the men and women who pursue excellence in one of the most challenging careers in sales...professional in-home selling.

Contents:

Preface

Let me tell you why I decided to write this book. The reason is very simple. I really like and respect salespeople – especially those who do in-home selling. And I'd like to see them earn more money and get greater satisfaction from their work. It's as simple as that.

I started my own career as a salesperson – and have sold for manufacturers, wholesalers, dealers – and of course for myself.

Since I began training salespeople full-time in 1997 I have had the chance to interface with literally thousands of sellers – some young, some old, some new, some experienced, some successful, some not so much. And here is my most important observation: the vast majority of these salespeople do what they do in a fairly 'unconscious' way. In other words, the best sellers are often 'unconsciously competent.' They do their thing and it works for them – often as a result of great, natural personal interaction skills. And the weakest salespeople are 'unconsciously incompetent.' They really can't analyze exactly what they are doing, or what they would need to practice to do better.

I would like to see every salesperson who leaves my training be more 'consciously competent.' In other words my training philosophy has always been that for people to perform a task they first need to understand how and why the task is best performed in a certain way; then they need to practice the task; then they need to apply that knowledge and practice on the job. And as they practice using the new skill on the job they gradually become 'consciously competent' on this skill. They know why it's done a certain way. They know how it's done correctly. And they have practiced enough to make the new skill their own. Now they can do the new skill correctly. And if at some point they're not getting the results they want, they have the underlying knowledge to go back and self analyze what they are doing, and what needs to be done differently. They are 'consciously competent' sellers.

So that's why I wrote this book. I want you to do better. I want you to make more money. I want you to enjoy your work and get satisfaction from it. And I believe the best way I can do this is to explain to you as clearly as I can exactly what the most successful salespeople do, why they do what they do, and to provide you with as much suggested practice as we reasonably can in book format.

This book is organized around the key concepts and skills that I believe are necessary for every in-home seller. I've tried to make it applicable to beginners who have never sold in the home – and still make it useful to you even if you have sold for decades.

Selling, in my opinion, is one of the most under appreciated jobs people do. Done correctly, it is as complex and challenging a task as any we can think of. The best salespeople are product experts, communications experts, strategic planners, and experts in reading and influencing human behavior. Anyone who does this job well should have a tremendous sense of accomplishment and personal satisfaction. I have tried to emphasize in this book the most professional aspects of selling, and my hope is that reading it will give you a renewed sense of pride and accomplishment – as well as motivate you to become a more complete salesperson.

I sincerely hope that at some point I will have the chance to meet you personally in a training session. In the meantime, feel free to check out my website at **www.sellingtrust.com**. You may email me your questions or comments, sign up for my monthly e-newsletter, or obtain copies of other in-home training materials including an instructional DVD of an in-home sales call using the T.R.U.S.T.® process.

CHAPTER 1

Why Do Customers Buy? If You Think You Know You're Probably Wrong!

I'm going to start this book by talking to you about 'mindset.' I'm going to make the point that the way you think about your customers will have more impact on your selling success than any other single factor. Your mindset will determine how you behave, how well you listen and what you say. Everything in this book is intended to help you create a mindset that will maximize your potential.

I got my first big job selling in 1975 and have never looked back with regret. Over the last almost 35 years, I've had the opportunity to sell to manufacturers, to wholesalers, to dealers and to consumers. I even had a brief stint as an independent small business owner. (That's how I learned about the impact of economic downturns on small businesses.) Even though I've been training other people since 1997, I still look at that as a form of selling. "*Would you like to buy my ideas?*"

I've enjoyed it all and wouldn't have wanted a different career.

Being an analytical kind of guy, I've given a lot of thought to why it is that I like selling. What is it that allows me to get up and treat every new day, every new customer, or every new trainee interaction with anticipation and enthusiasm? When so many people around me are not enjoying what they do, why the heck am I having such a good time?

And it's not just me either. Every week I meet people who are equally engaged and enthusiastic about what they are doing. Why do so many of us love what we are doing, while so many others merely tolerate – or even dread – the 'daily grind.'

Here's at least part of the answer.

There are two fundamentally different kinds of work. In one type of job, we learn at the beginning how to do a task, and then we are expected to repeat the task more or less the same way every time. We learn how to cook the burger or assemble the machine during a period of training, and then we're supposed to cook the burger or assemble the machine the same way each time. Some people like this kind of work. They are comfortable with the predictable repetition – and may even gain great satisfaction from a job well done. And I'm not just talking about fast food or assembly jobs. Many highly paid and complex jobs are like this. Flying airplanes. Fixing teeth. Maintaining equipment. These are all great jobs. But they're characterized by intensive initial training, and consistent and predictable on-the-job actions.

The second kind of work involves learning basic concepts at the beginning, but then being faced with one unique and unpredictable situation after another. Selling is a great example of this kind of job. We can learn basic selling skills – but every customer interaction is going to be different. When we walk into the buyer's office, or when we ring that customer's door bell, we have no idea what we're going to run into.

There are many jobs like this – managing a business or a department, owning a small business, teaching or coaching a group of students, etc.

The fact is that some people do much better, and are much happier, in jobs where the rules, procedures, and outcomes are very predictable. And other people do much better, and are much happier, in jobs where there is continuous uncertainty.

I'm one of the latter.

A consultant and trainer named Larry Wilson used to use the analogy of the trapeze acrobat. The most exciting part of the acrobat's job is the time between when he lets go of one trapeze, but hasn't yet caught the other trapeze.

Some people think about that analogy and think, "*Wow, what a rush!*" Other people think about it and think, "*No way, man!*"

Two points.

First, I'm not being evaluative at all here. I know some really happy dentists. I just wouldn't want to do that myself. And I'm pretty sure they wouldn't be comfortable doing what I do – facing unique situations every day. Anybody who does a job well can be proud. But some of us can be happy in more predictable jobs, and some of us like that trapeze analogy.

Second, I understand that this distinction between more routine jobs and jobs that are less predictable is not always that cut and dried. A lot of routine jobs have plenty of room for creativity, and a lot of more unpredictable jobs have their routine aspects. I know that I personally have spent an awful lot of time sitting in tedious sales meetings, and a lot of time just sitting and studying product spec sheets.

But I believe my general point is valid. I love selling because it is unpredictable. The more challenging the situation, the more I enjoy it.

If you are the type of person who embraces... who thrives on... unique challenges, then you can love selling even more than you do now. The secret is to emphasize the uniqueness of each sales interaction and de-emphasize the routine aspects of what we have to get done.

I not only want you to be good at selling, I want you to love selling. I want you to be able to get up every day and say, "*This is my opportunity to get out and do something that I do well, and that I really enjoy.*"

If you do love routine, and hate unpredictable situations, you're probably not going to enjoy a life in sales. And, as hard as it is for me to say it, you probably will be happier if you investigate other career choices.

But if you love a challenge, and like not knowing exactly what's going to happen next, then you can have a great and enjoyable selling career. And the methods I'm going to teach you will not only make you more effective, but they will help you get greater joy and satisfaction from your career.

SO… WHY DO CUSTOMERS BUY?

Why do customers buy?

That was the first question that our sales trainer asked in the very first sales training I attended more than 30 years ago. As I said, I went to work for a large manufacturing company in the mid-1970s, and they sent me to their version of 'Selling 101.' Following introductions, our trainer declared that we needed to start at the beginning – and that means a discussion of the question, "*Why do people buy?*"

Our trainer further went on to teach us that there was an **answer** to that question – and that the answer was that **customers buy to satisfy needs**. In the language of selling, it is product or service **benefits** that satisfy needs... so we needed to learn about, and to practice, selling benefits. And with that we were into our first lesson on doing benefit selling. Here is the product. Here are the features. Here are the benefits. Please memorize all that… there's going to be a test.

I actually enjoyed that training. And I learned a lot of basic skills that I still use and teach today. But after 30 years, I can look back now and say that my thinking about selling, and the thinking of many of my sales training peers, has evolved. I can even go so far as to say that the way we were taught selling might have even given me some bad habits that took years to break. I'm going to try to save you that time.

In that training three decades ago, the focus was on developing **our skills as salespeople**. Customers have needs; therefore we need to be able to do effective benefits selling; here's how we do that; let's practice these new skills. Then we went on from benefit selling to making effective demonstrations, objection handling, closing, even some pretty sophisticated stuff on business-to-business selling.

The only problem with the training was that as soon as I got back home and went out to call on real customers, they didn't always behave like they were supposed to! They were busy, or they were angry about something, or they had business problems that I wasn't equipped to solve… or a thousand other distractions.

Now I look back and realize that I had been taught what **salespeople** are supposed to do – and I didn't know enough about what **customers** do.

My whole reason for writing this book is to try to help you learn at least some of the lessons I had to learn the hard way by trial and error. And the very first lesson is the most important one. **Selling success is not just about your ability to present a product, handle an objection, and ask for an order. Rather, it is about your ability to read people, to relate to people, and to get people to T.R.U.S.T.® you**.

People are unique. Every person is different.

Houses, on the other hand, are not all that unique. In any given region of the country one $350,000 home is going to look pretty much like any other $350,000 home. Similar equipment, systems, construction, materials.

But the **homeowners** are going to be completely different – young, old, married, single, financially sound, financially shaky, outgoing, introverted, happy, cranky, knowledgeable, clueless, technical, non-technical, forward, passive... and so on.

Now, I've already told you that if you want to increase your love of selling, you need to deemphasize the routine aspects and emphasize the **uniqueness** of each situation. For in-home sellers, the implications of this are clear. The houses are fairly routine; the homeowners themselves are unique. Deemphasize the structures. Emphasize your ability to work with the homeowner.

So let's ask the question again, "*Why do people buy?*"

The old answer – "*People buy because they have needs, benefits satisfy needs, so let's learn to sell benefits*" – just doesn't do it. Another way to answer the question is this, "*Customers are individuals; individuals do things for different reasons; therefore we don't know exactly why a particular customer is going to buy.*"

If we put our two answers together we get this, "*Customers buy because they have needs; but because no two customers are exactly the same, we can't know why any particular customer might buy. It would be up to the salesperson to find out what the customer's exact needs are.*"

That's actually a pretty good answer.

PEOPLE DO HAVE GENERIC NEEDS

We can easily put down a list of **generic** needs. Here's one for starters:

- Save money / increase wealth
- Save work / avoid problems
- Save time
- Increase self esteem
- Increase security
- Increase peace of mind

But these are just that – generic needs. We have a generic need to save time – but I've met people who heat their homes with hand split wood. Their time is less valuable than their money. I have a neighbor who pays people to put in and tend her flower garden. She likes gardening, but her time is more important than saving money.

I could write an entire book on the last generic item alone – increased peace of mind. This is probably the most important generic need for in-home sales people to think about. (And we will come back to it again in other chapters.) Entire industries – life insurance, auto insurance, smoke and CO detection, home security, etc. – are there to provide nothing but peace of mind. But beyond that, peace of mind gets tied up with all kinds of other benefit questions like, "*How do I know I'll get the savings or quality promised?*" or "*How do I know I won't be cheated?*" or "*How do I know that what I'm being told is true?*"

The point here is this: even though most people share generic needs to some degree, we have no way of knowing how an **individual** customer views those needs. How important is one relative to another? Which ones are most important? Which are not important at all?

IT'S THE INDIVIDUAL NEEDS THAT ARE IMPORTANT

The fact is that no two people are the same, and so no two people can ever have the same exact needs. Sure, people who buy cars share a generic need for transportation to get them around town, but people buy cars for $500 and they buy cars for $100,000. People need a kitchen sink so the water goes somewhere, but people buy $50 sinks and people buy $1,000 sinks. All people need peace of mind, but some people buy life insurance, and other people think it's a poor investment.

In my selling seminars I often start by asking people to tell the group about the best thing they have ever bought. What did they buy that they really think is high-quality, works like they had hoped, and was worth what they paid?

I've had answers that range from fishhooks to front loading washers to snowmobiles to big screen TVs. And guess what? It's **never** the basic model. No one has ever told me that the best thing they ever bought was the cheapest, most stripped-down, generic thing available. And guess what else? A significant number of their peers in the class would **never** pay as much as they paid for the same product. The conversations are usually something like this, "*Well I'd never pay $800 for a washing machine, but sure, I'd pay $300 for a golf club.*"

People are complicated. They have different personalities. They have different backgrounds. They are at different levels on the socio-economic scale. They're in different circumstances.

And this is why we know that the answer to the question "*Why do customers buy?*" is "*I don't know!*" I don't know because I don't know any one customer's background, situation, personality, or internal wants and desires!

AN OPEN-MINDED MINDSET CAN MAKE THE DIFFERENCE BETWEEN 'AVERAGE' AND 'EXCEPTIONAL' PERFORMANCE

Salespeople can approach a new client with one of three different mindsets. Read these three brief scenarios.

John. John sells heating and air-conditioning. He believes that all of his customers want essentially the same thing – a basic system correctly installed at a low price. He feels that his primary role is to do an accurate survey and system layout, and to present a competitive bid.

Phil. Phil sells heating and air-conditioning. He believes that he can read a customer's needs based on his personal impressions of the customer, and his observations during his home survey. He will suggest system upgrades and enhancements based on observations about home value, type of car driven, quality of home decor, etc.

Rick. Rick sells heating and air-conditioning. He believes each customer is unique, and that his customers may not have sufficient information to know exactly what they would like in a system. He believes one of his primary roles is to find out how his customers view different needs, and to educate each customer as needed so that the customer can understand and evaluate choices available to them.

The **mindset** of each salesperson will drive that salesperson's behavior.

John and Phil will spend relatively little time with the homeowner, moving quickly on to the job survey. Rick, on the other hand, will need to spend significant time with the homeowner because he needs to find out what they know, or do not know, and what they want, or do not want.

We know that Rick is right. But when I work with salespeople I meet a lot more 'Johns' and 'Phils' that I do 'Ricks.' John and Phil could be intelligent, hard-working guys, but their mindset is causing them to do the wrong things. It is their **mindset** – not a lack of skills – that prevents them from spending time with the customer. And, it is their mindset which will prevent them from ever achieving optimal success.

Rick might be no smarter or harder working, but his **mindset** is causing him to do the right thing. Because he believes that all customers are different, and because he believes he can't uncover these differences except through talking with the customer, he has the potential to be more successful.

Rick is also much more likely to enjoy what he is doing, and to find his career truly rewarding, just as John is the most likely to find his job routine and not rewarding.

I want you to understand that it can be your choice how much satisfaction – and success – you get from your work.

I know that if you stopped reading this book right now, but accepted what I've just said about mindset – that it could dramatically increase your sales output and career satisfaction.

In every industry I can think of, the top sellers don't just sell a little more than the average sellers. They sell **times** more. If you show me a business where the average salesperson sells $500,000 per year, I'll find you a salesperson who's doing more than $1 million. That's not just a difference in product knowledge, selling skills, or hard work. My experience is that top sellers simply think differently about what they do. They are like Rick in my example. They don't assume things. They don't believe that all people want is price. They do believe that people are individuals who want to be treated as just that – individuals. They believe that many people, if they're simply educated on what is possible, will want more than the most basic system.

The best salespeople do the best job of relating to the most customers. All of us get along well with people who are just like us. Top salespeople have figured out a way to relate to just about everybody! This is because they have a **mindset** that each customer is an individual and each customer therefore needs to be **treated** as a unique individual.

THE T.R.U.S.T.® SELLING MODEL

A few years ago I trademarked the name T.R.U.S.T.® selling. Here's what **T.R.U.S.T.®** stands for:

- **T** is for Truth
- **R** is for Relationship
- **U** is for Understanding
- **S** is for Show choices
- **T** is for Take action

In T.R.U.S.T.® selling we **talk to the customer**. Asking questions and listening to the customer's responses gives us a clear **Understanding** of the customer's situation and thinking. And, it develops a **Relationship** with the customer. That's how relationships are developed... through dialogue. Once we have a clear understanding of the customer's needs, we can **Show** the customer what is possible and help them **Take action**. And at every stage we use **Truthfulness** as the only acceptable measure of the information we provide to the customer.

Many approaches to in-home selling are designed to accomplish one goal – walk out with an order.

T.R.U.S.T.® selling is designed to accomplish not just one but **three distinct results**.

First, it is designed to **get an order**. When homeowners invite salespeople into their homes, they're obviously looking for someone they can trust (Truth); they are looking for someone they can relate to (Relationship); they're looking for someone who can advise them on their particular situation (Understand / Show choices); they're looking for a real solution (Take action). T.R.U.S.T.® selling is what people want; **it produces exceptionally high close rates**.

Second, T.R.U.S.T.® selling is designed to **increase the dollars per sale**. Did you know that under the right circumstances only about 20% of people will opt for the cheapest solution? About 20% of customers buy the cheapest model, about 20% buy the best (and most expensive) model, and about 60% buy in the middle. This is true for cars or cameras, clothes or beer. As long as the consumer can see clearly all the choices available to them, the majority will pick the middle and upper level models. In most retail environments, you can easily see the choices available. If you go into Best Buy you can instantly see the good, better, and best big-screen TVs, cameras, and phones, whatever. Just knowing that there is a $4,000 model makes it more likely that you'll buy the $2,000 model… even if you could also opt for the $1,000 bargain model. But in in-home selling, customers may see only the low-end model that is presented by the in-home seller. T.R.U.S.T.® sellers **show** choices. Even if they believe that the customer is very price sensitive, they still make sure the customer is educated on all the models that are available. In-home sellers who only sell the basic model will sell 100% basic models. In-home sellers who show choices will, over time, sell about 20% basic models, 20% deluxe models and 60% in the mid-range. You can do the numbers for yourself!

The third thing that T.R.U.S.T.® selling is designed to do is to **secure future business**.

THERE IS A LINK BETWEEN SELLING SUCCESS AND REFERRALS

A key difference between average and top performers is that top sellers get a large portion of their leads from referrals. In other words, not only do they sell more, but they end up with more satisfied customers, and these satisfied customers refer friends and relatives to the salesperson.

If I get a cold lead, the chances of my closing that are going to be about 40 to 50% if I really do a good job. But, if I get a referral, my chances of closing jump dramatically – maybe as high as 90%. I've been referred by a friend. I very likely do not have a competitor bidding. The customer is looking for someone to help them buy – not just give them a low bid.

Maybe you are already starting to see the obvious linkages between **mindset, selling success,** and **referrals**.

If your mindset is that each customer is a unique individual, and that causes you to spend **more time** talking with the customer about their needs, wants, and desires, two things happen.

First, you start to develop **a relationship** with the customer! Relationships arise from talking to people! The stronger your relationship with the customer, the greater the chances are that the customer will begin to **trust** you.

Second, by spending more time talking to the customer, you are going to **uncover more information** about the customer, and you can therefore offer a better, more customized solution to the customer's needs – whether those needs are product related, financial, or even personal.

In other words, your chances of meeting or exceeding the customer's expectations go up dramatically as you spend more time with the customer.

Now, let me tie all this together for you.

About 40 years ago, companies in the United States started to embrace the so-called 'quality process.' The idea behind the quality process is that it costs less to **avoid problems** than it does to fix them, and also that it is less expensive to **keep good customers** than it is to go out and get new ones. Boy, as I look around it sure seems like some companies have forgotten this! But even if companies don't always act the way we'd like, they still understand the fundamental truths of the quality process, including the idea that a company's least expensive new business comes from its existing customers.

It's really important for any in-home salesperson to understand how this principle actually works in in-home selling.

Prior to the quality process, most companies felt that all they needed to do was to offer products or services that **met** the customer's expectations. If customers expected to replace the tires on the car about every 40,000 miles, and your company offered a value priced 40,000-mile tire, then your customers would continue to buy from you. They would be 'satisfied' enough to stay with you. And, that's great until someone comes along with a tire that lasts 60,000 miles! The new competitor comes in and **exceeds the customer's current expectations** – and takes away your business.

If you are old enough to remember back 30 years, (or go ahead and ask your Dad), compare some of your expectations from then to your expectations today. We used to expect a one-week package delivery; long-distance calling was a weekend luxury; coffee came two ways – black or with cream and sugar; fruits and vegetables were only available in season; film processing took several days; and so on.

Business moves from one company to another when one company figures out how to **not just meet** the customer's expectations – but to **exceed** the customer's expectations.

Here is what we know about customer behavior as a result of research arising from the quality process:

- If we **meet** a customer's expectations – that customer may or may not continue to do business with our company, and may or may not refer others to us.

- If we **exceed** a customer's expectations – that customer will continue to do business with our company, and will refer other business to us if the opportunity arises.

- If we fail to meet a customer's expectations – that customer will not do business with us again, and will actively tell others about our failure if the opportunity arises.

In in-home selling, here is what customers generally expect:

- That the salesperson will know what they are talking about.
- That the salesperson will be reasonably polite.
- That the salesperson will make a fair, competitive proposal.

Customers do not generally expect that the salesperson will come into their homes, ask questions and listen carefully to responses, present careful explanations of various options, and treat the homeowner as an individual with unique needs that need to be probed. But, of course, this is exactly what needs to be done.

In-home sellers who exceed their customer's expectations will have a greater proportion of customers who will call them again should the need arise, and who will refer other new business to them!

BUILDING RELATIONSHIPS WITH PEOPLE IS A SKILL

People often talk about the ability to relate to others as a God-given talent... something you're just born with. We hear people say things like, "*People sure like Frank don't they? He's such a nice guy... everybody likes him.*" And obviously, there's an element of truth here. Some people are born with likable personalities. They are just naturally warm and outgoing. They seem to know what to say to put people at ease. People do just like them.

If you were born with that kind of personality... that's really great. This can truly enhance your selling success. But my point here is this. I can think of dozens of top sellers who I have known who might not fit the 'warm and cuddly' profile – but who nonetheless possess the skills necessary to relate to people effectively in selling situations.

Just for the record, I might point out that I also have known a lot of 'warm and cuddly,' very likable folks who don't reach their full potential as salespeople due to a lack of some skill or other, or due to some other issue… like an inability to develop the optimum mindset!

Relationships are built on **trust**. Trust is developed through **open, honest dialogue**. In other words, effective working relationships between you and your customers are an **outcome** of your skills in communicating. Questioning skills... listening skills... and speaking skills... combined with openness, honesty, and empathy for your customers.

For me, the proof of this is in my own experience. The best sellers I know run the entire gamut from warm personality, with excellent communication skills, to cool personality, also with excellent communication skills. **Communication skills, not personality, are the common denominator for excellent sellers**.

THE BASIS FOR GOOD COMMUNICATION SKILLS IS UNDERSTANDING PEOPLE

I hope this opening chapter has at least convinced you that skills in reading people are just as important as product knowledge and selling skills like benefit selling, closing, and objection handling (which we fully intend to cover in the later chapters of this book). That's why we started this book at the **customer**.

Now, stick with me for one more chapter about customers. In Chapter 2, we're going to take a look at some of the important ways that customers do differ from one another – and which of those differences are most important to your selling success.

CHAPTER 2

Think Like Your Customer: Understanding Human Behavior In Selling

In Chapter 1 I told you how important it is to have the right **mindset**, and that each customer is, in fact, **unique**. Two homeowners living in the same neighborhood, even side-by-side, in essentially identical houses, are going to be very different individuals.

We are all different. How would you feel if someone came into your home and treated you as a 'type' – as in, "*I know your type?*" Suppose that cars were sold by in-home salespeople. Let's say a car salesperson came to your home, looked around a little bit, and then told you, "*Your kind of people usually gets a stripped down minivan. Here's a quote on one. Give me a call if you want to move ahead.*" Making assumptions and judgments about others isn't fair or appropriate and it certainly isn't an effective sales strategy.

Most in-home salespeople sell things that can't be sold in a retail store environment. Someone... a salesperson... has to actually go into the home, assess the situation, and take measurements and price out the job. Today's products and services are offered with a variety of features and quality.

Almost everything we sell has at least a good – better – best choice. There are also related accessories and other services we can offer. It's not possible to guess or judge what people will or won't want, or can or can't afford.

Just think about what you **don't** know about a customer when you first greet them:

- You **don't** know why they contacted you.
- You **don't** know if you are the only supplier contacted or are one of many.
- You **don't** know what this customer may have heard about your company, or what preconceived notions they may have about you.
- You **don't** know if they are looking for an excellent solution that is a good value or for a rock-bottom price.
- You **don't** know what their financial situation is.
- You **don't** know how they make decisions.
- You **don't** know how technical or non-technical they might be.
- You **don't** know how they feel about issues such as energy savings, security, peace of mind, etc.
- You **don't** know how long they might live in their home.

If you start to think about what you don't know about the customer you're going to realize that the items fall into two different categories. First we don't know the **situational** stuff about the customer... their home, their family, their finances, their future intentions. Second, we don't know **personal** stuff about the customer... what the customer is like as an individual.

I've already introduced you to the **T.R.U.S.T.®** selling model. Think for a minute about the **R**... relationship, and the **U**... understanding. Using questions to gain an understanding of the customer's needs also builds the relationship that you have with the customer. The existence of a relationship feeds our ability to gain a deeper understanding of the customer and the more we understand and relate to the customer the better the relationship becomes. It's a loop... **a closed loop**.

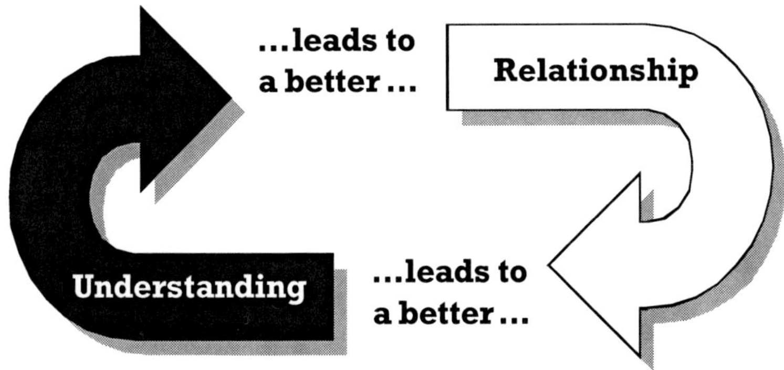

Questions lead to **understanding**. The resulting dialogue builds a stronger **relationship**. The existence of a **relationship** allows us to gain a deeper **understanding**.

It's easy to find out situational stuff about the customer. We just ask. "*Why did you call us? What ideas do you have about what you would like to have? What is your schedule?*"

It's harder to get at the more personal stuff. We learn the more personal stuff as a result of our engagement... our growing **relationship**... with the customer.

YOU DON'T NEED A DEGREE IN PSYCHOLOGY...

You don't need a degree in psychology to be a good salesperson, but the more you study and understand how people behave, beginning with yourself, the more effective you will be in all your relationships, including your relationships with your potential customers. Since people are different it would not make sense to treat everyone as though they are all the same.

I want to give you some insight into two aspects of human thinking and behavior that are important in selling. The first of these is the area of **human needs**. People clearly view wants and needs differently from one another. For example, some buy the basic model and some want the premium model. We'll take a look at how individuals differ in the way they view wants and needs and how those views factor into their decisions.

The second area is that of **personal styles**. You have a style and so do I. The way you prevent differences in styles from becoming an issue, and the way you capitalize on similarities in styles can produce a significant sales advantage for you.

ONE WAY TO LOOK AT NEEDS

During the 1940s, a psychologist named Abraham Maslow developed a model that he called a 'hierarchy of needs.' That model is sound enough, and simple enough, that it is still being used today. Maslow identified five levels of human needs.

Level 1 **Physiological Needs**
The most basic needs for food, water, air, etc. to stay alive.

Level 2 **Safety / Security Needs**
The need for physical and mental security, such as a safe environment in which to live, financial security, job security, etc.

Level 3 **Social or Belonging Needs**
The need for family, friends, community, etc.

Level 4 **Esteem Needs**
The need for recognition, reward, and leadership within the group.

Level 5 **Self Actualization Needs**
The need to achieve one's full potential – truth, wisdom, meaning, etc.

Maslow actually put these in a hierarchy like this...

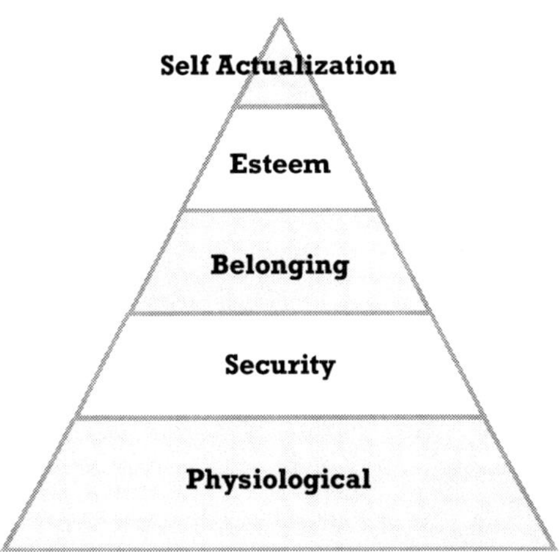

He theorized that humans move upward in the hierarchy as lower-level needs are fulfilled. In other words, once I feel **secure**, then I can worry about my place in the **group**, and having taken care of that, I can focus on my position of **esteem** within the group.

Later research has discounted the hierarchical nature of the model. There are just too many exceptions; people are too complicated to fit into any one model. Did you see the movie "Into the Wild?" It's about a young man who gives up safety and security and dies trying to 'self actualize' in the wilds of Alaska. Consider the person who buys expensive clothing to fit into a peer group while at the same time struggling to pay his rent. The hierarchy aspect just doesn't hold up.

But I still like the model because I think Maslow did a nice job of identifying the **kinds of needs** that people have in very simple, easy to remember terms. As Americans, our physiological needs – clean air and water, a basic food supply – are pretty much taken care of. Given that, in any particular sales situation people will tend to be oriented toward the higher needs including security, belonging, esteem and self actualization.

Let's take this example. Let's say you sell a product that saves energy and therefore reduces utility costs. Why would someone want to buy that? If your first thought is that people just need to save money you could be overlooking a huge portion of the total sales opportunity.

For people with strong **security needs:**

These people would be the ones in search of the dollars savings. Perhaps they are on a fixed income. Perhaps they are overextended. At any rate, a return on investment story might have impact. Also, emphasizing exceptional warranties or an outstanding track record with a product will have meaning and value to this person.

For people with strong **social / belonging needs:**

These people might be influenced by the behavior of their peer group. For example, "*Nearly 100% of my customers settle on the more energy efficient model.*" They may be influenced by some overall social effort. "The governor has asked us all to help reduce energy consumption in the state, and this can be an important part of that effort."

For people with **strong esteem needs**:

These people might be influenced by the opportunity to show leadership. "*Eventually everyone will embrace this technology, but right now it's a real opportunity to be on the cutting edge.*" They may also be influenced by the one-ups-manship potential. "*You'd have the satisfaction of knowing that no one has a more efficient unit.*"

For people with strong **self actualization needs:**

These people might embrace an energy savings opportunity simply out of the desire to do what is best. "*No product does more to help save the environment than this one.*"

So how do you know which approach to take? Well, the simple answer is you don't. When you first meet a customer, she doesn't have a label on her forehead that says, "*I have strong esteem needs.*" You need to find that out **by talking with and listening to the customer.**

I might point out that this is not about economics. Some rich people just want the least expensive solution. Some poor people want to save the world.

I have friends who were approaching retirement and who were going to build a modest retirement home. These folks were financially comfortable but certainly not wealthy. They had a strong environmental commitment and as a result planned to build their home primarily with certified harvested lumber. The first builder they talked to responded, "*You don't want to do that. That would add a lot of unnecessary cost.*" The second builder responded, "*You don't want to do that. That would just complicate things and might delay the schedule.*" The third builder they talked to said, "*Of course we can do that. I admire your commitment to using green methods. Would you like me to provide you information on some other green building options that we could do for you?*"

So which builder do you think got the job?

Builder number one assumes that everyone wants the least expensive home. Builder number two assumes that people also want to avoid anything that slows things up. Builder number three **doesn't assume** anything. Builder number three knows that it's his job to get a sense of what the customer needs (wants) and do his absolute best to give it to them. Builder number three has the **mindset** that I talked about in Chapter 1 – the mindset that it's his job to help each customer understand the various choices that are available and to help them get the best ones **for them**.

In summary, the Maslow model gives you four pretty easy-to-remember basic kinds of customers:

1. Those who are very concerned about basic security. "*What's the safest thing to do?*"
2. Those who are very concerned about social implications. "*What are the Joneses doing?*"
3. Those who are very concerned about status and esteem issues. "*Am I the first?*"
4. Those who are very concerned about doing what they feel is most important. "*What do I really want to do?*"

Money and social status clearly affect this, but there is more to it than that. The only way to get a sense for where the customer is coming from is to listen to them. Once you have an understanding of the customer's needs you can focus your sales proposal to meet those specific needs.

You could take a couple of minutes at this point and try to make a list of the kinds of sales points that might be important to each of the four kinds of customers. Then compare your list to mine below.

SALES POINTS RELATED TO SAFETY / SECURITY NEEDS

- Energy savings, as related to return on investment
- Quality as related to long life
- Quality as related to fewer repairs
- Warranties
- Financing / low monthly cost
- Brand recognition / reliability
- Contractor reputation
- Testimonials from other customers regarding reliability of product or contractor
- Proof, such as third-party testing, measured data, etc.
- Post sale follow-up actions
- Personal referrals
- Employee screening programs, especially drug testing

SALES POINTS RELATED TO SOCIAL / BELONGING NEEDS

- Brand reputation
- Contractor reputation
- Surveys / studies on popularity of product
- Surveys on popularity of contractor
- Local testimonials
- Personal referrals
- Energy savings as related to group norms

SALES POINTS RELATED TO ESTEEM NEEDS

- Customized solutions
- Brand reputation / premium brand
- Reputation of contractor among affluent buyers
- Premium features
- Testimonials / case studies from affluent buyers
- Newest technology
- Personal service
- Access to contractor's owners / leadership
- Post sale follow-up
- Priority after sale service programs
- Featuring job in the company's sales materials
- Energy savings as a leadership issue

SALES POINTS RELATED TO SELF ACTUALIZATION NEEDS

- Energy savings as a greater social good; reducing one's carbon footprint
- Reputation of contractor as a community leader
- Contractor's ability to respond to unique requirements

CUSTOMERS ALSO HAVE UNIQUE PERSONAL STYLES

The other aspect of customer behavior that salespeople need to be aware of is what I'll call personal styles.

An obvious example of personal style differences would be an introvert versus an extrovert. Introverted people are more comfortable being out of the limelight while extroverted people like being the center of attention.

A **personal style** like this is different from the **needs perception** that we just talked about. We could have two older retired gentlemen, both on fixed income, and both very concerned about basic financial security. One of these gentlemen may be introverted and the other is extroverted. They share a common view of basic needs but they have different personal styles.

THERE ARE THREE IMPORTANT STYLE ELEMENTS

If you are really interested in personal styles you can buy many books or attend any number of training sessions that use various models to analyze styles. Some of these get quite complicated. What I'll do is help you focus on just a few style elements that can quickly help you be more effective in in-home selling. Here are three:

1. Introverted versus extroverted
2. Strong-willed versus passive
3. Detail oriented versus big picture oriented

Here is why these are important. Your job is to find out what the customer needs and wants and provide choices that meet those expectations. This requires dialogue between you and the customer. The effectiveness of that dialogue is going to depend on how the customer **feels** about you. If the customer **trusts** you and **feels comfortable** chatting with you you'll get good information. You'll also establish a rapport that strengthens the **relationship** that you have with the customer.

If you are too forward with an introverted customer, that person may withdraw from your perceived aggressiveness. If you are too introverted yourself with a very extroverted customer, that person may feel you lack confidence.

In the same way, you will not optimize your relationship with your customer if…

- You gloss over the details of your product or offering with a detail oriented person.

- You overwhelm a non-technical customer with excessive detail.
- You get into a clash of wills with a strong-willed customer.
- You fail to provide gentle guidance to a very passive customer.

HOW IMPORTANT IS THE ISSUE OF PERSONAL STYLES?

For each personal style characteristic there is a scale that goes between two extremes. Here are the scales for the three characteristics:

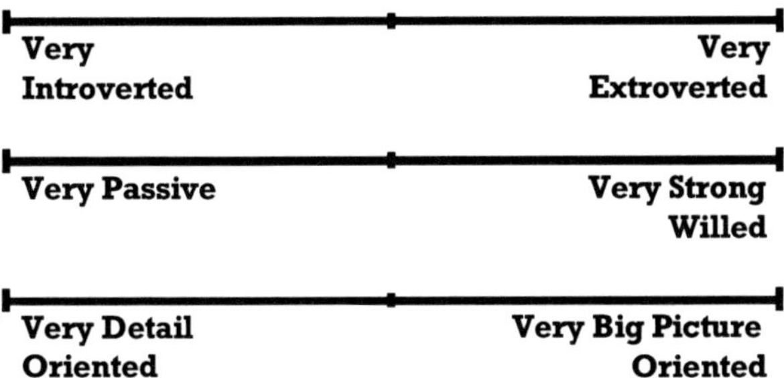

Few people are at the extremes on any scale. Most are going to be inclined to be on one side or the other of the middle. If a customer is strongly oriented toward one end of a scale, you will want to adjust appropriately. If **you** are strongly oriented toward one end of a scale, you will want to be aware of that and also adjust appropriately.

What do I mean by adjust appropriately? Well, you can't change your basic personality, but you can adjust your behavior.

When your styles clash, this is not the customer's problem… it is **your** problem. You can only be in the top 5% of all sellers in your field if you can effectively sell to everyone.

You can see intuitively that this is really most important when either you or the customer has a more extreme style, or when you and the customer lean strongly in opposite directions on one scale.

I suggest you take a minute and try to honestly assess your own style on each of these three scales.

- Are you strongly introverted or strongly extroverted?
- Are you very strong-willed or very passive?
- Are you very detail oriented or very big picture oriented?

I recognize, by the way, that very few passive folks stumble into in-home selling, but it is not unlikely that some sellers are going to be quite strong willed. Here are the most common conditions I run into with in-home salespeople I've met, and a few practical suggestions.

If you are... somewhat introverted:

In some industries either technicians are asked to sell, or former technicians become salespeople or even business owners. And it is possible that some of these folks may be more comfortable with the product than with the customers. This is not a major issue. Customers inherently trust knowledgeable people. But there are a few steps you can take to be a bit more outgoing. For each call, get yourself focused on your introduction. Try to use eye contact and a firm handshake. Consciously raise your voice somewhat. Use active listening skills. (These are covered in detail in Chapter 5.) In general, concentrate on staying focused on the customer, and on keeping your energy level up.

If you are... somewhat extroverted:

People normally enjoy dealing with extroverts. That way they know the conversation will keep going! But make sure that you are adhering to the 'customer talks most' rule. If you sense that you are talking more than the customer, bring yourself back to questions. I'll talk more about this in Chapter 5 as well.

If you are... a bit too technical:

Here is the rule for presenting technical information. Start with the big picture, preferably using simple analogies to make yourself clear. Then ask the customer if they would like more data. If the answer is no, then go on.

Here's a sample: "*Given what you've told me, I'd suggest that we look at this medium efficiency model. We have units that are rated both more and less efficient, but this model provides good value for your dollar. If you were buying a car, this would be like the 25-mile-per gallon model. I could give you higher efficiency, but it would cost more. Would you like me to go into more detail on comparing efficiency?*"

If you are... pretty strong-willed:

Selling requires a determination to get results. Your job is to move customers to action. But, remember that in **T.R.U.S.T.®** selling we want every sales interaction to result in two things. First, we would like the customer to say yes to our proposal. And second, we'd like the customer to feel confident that they made the right decision – so confident that they would call you again, or recommend you to other potential customers.

If your customers perceive what you call 'drive' as what they might call 'pushiness,' you might get the order, but lose the long-term potential – the very satisfied customer who will call you back and will refer other customers to you. If you're getting a lot of referrals, you're obviously okay. But if you're not getting referrals, and you do have a strong personality, you need to assess this. This is admittedly a very tricky area. I personally do not have a lot of respect for salespeople who do not do what they are paid to do – and that is to work very hard to earn the customer's business, and then ask for the order. That's just professional determination. 'Pushy' to me goes beyond that into talking too much, interrupting, and arguing with the customer. If you're not sure if your personality is a bit too strong for some of your customers, ask your boss or another experienced salesperson for some feedback.

HOW ABOUT CUSTOMERS WITH STRONG PERSONAL STYLES?

If you follow the **T.R.U.S.T.®** process and develop and use the tools and techniques covered in the remaining chapters of this book, you are going to gain an understanding of the customer's personal style by the time you make your proposal.

As with your own personal style, this really only becomes an issue if the customer's style is fairly extreme, or if it clashes with your own style.

More than 90% of the time it's just not going to be an issue. You'll ask questions, the customer will respond openly, and a working relationship will develop. You'll be able to concentrate on understanding the customer's needs and desires, and then producing a proposal that fits those needs and desires.

But on occasion, it will be an issue. You have to remember that the customer's personality 'problem' is actually **your** problem. Top sales people figure out how to work with essentially everybody... including 'jerks.' It's more important to earn the business and earn the referral than it is to be right. If the customer feels that they are more technically knowledgeable than you are – that's fine, as long as the job gets installed correctly in the end. If the customer insists that your pricing is out of line, that's okay. You might have to remove features from the proposal that would be good for the customer, but you can do that if necessary.

Chapter 7 in this book talks about bumps in the road – customer objections. Treat a personality conflict as a bump in the road. Read the material on disarming objections and use the technique actively. The phrase, "*I can see your point*" can go a long way in preventing problems.

CHAPTER 3

T.R.U.S.T.® Selling: Getting The Big Picture

<u>Every</u> sale has three phases.

It doesn't matter if you're selling submarines to the federal government or an automatic garage door to a homeowner – you have to go through the same three phases:

1. Understand what the customer's needs are.
2. Create appropriate solutions to those needs.
3. Show choices and gain agreement to take action – to close the deal.

I tell people that the definition of T.R.U.S.T.® selling is simple. In T.R.U.S.T.® selling, we find out what the customer wants and we give it to them!

That's really just a restatement of any good selling process isn't it? Find out what the customer wants – that's the needs analysis. Then give it to them – meaning show your solutions to the customer's needs and gain agreement to move ahead.

It's so simple in concept. So why is it hard to do in practice?

Do you remember John – my example salesperson in Chapter 1? John is the guy whose mindset is that all customers want more or less the same thing and that it's his job to make an accurate job survey and to deliver a competitive quote.

Here is what one of John's sales calls sounds like.

John: "*Mr. Jones? Hi, I'm John Smith from Acme Heating. I understand you folks called us regarding a quote on a new furnace?*"

Customer: "*Yes, that's correct.*"

John: "*Great. I'll be happy to help you with that. I'll need to check out your existing system and take some measurements. If you can show me where the equipment room is, we'll get started.*"

Customer: "*About how long will that take, John?*"

John: "*Oh, it should take no more than 30 minutes and I'll have a proposal to go over with you.*"

And with that, John is off to the equipment room. In 30 minutes he'll be back with a written proposal to show to Mr. Jones. Our scenario continues...

John: "*Well Mr. Jones, let me go over this proposal with you. I've done some calculations and I believe your old system is slightly oversized – plus equipment efficiencies have improved a lot in the last few years, – so I'm proposing our Binford Model 202 which is...*"

HEY WAIT… STOP! What's the deal here? John sounds like he's into the **second** phase of the selling process, which is to show his solution to the customer's needs. What happened to the **first** phase? What happened to understanding the customer's needs? Let me ask him what he's thinking...

Tom: *"Say, John, it seems like you might have missed something on this sales call – like the part where you determine the customer's needs."*

John: *"Well, Tom, I thought I did that. They called and said they needed a new furnace, so I knew that already. And I did a good survey of the job, so I thought my proposal was okay."*

Tom: *"But what about the Joneses themselves? What do you know about them?"*

John: *"What do you mean?"*

Tom: *"Well, remember in Chapter 1, I said that every customer is different? And in Chapter 2, I said that those differences affect the way people look at needs? And that they also have personal styles that might be important?"*

John: *"Yeah, I guess, but what else do I need to know? They just want a new furnace."*

Tom: *"Okay, here are a few things that I might want to know if I were you:*

- Why did they call you?
- Why are they replacing their furnace now?
- How do they like their current furnace?
- What don't they like about it?
- How do they feel about energy costs and savings?
- Have they made other kinds of system upgrades?
- How long do they plan to stay in this house?"

John: *"Hey wait, wait, wait. How am I supposed to find out all that? Jeez, that could take forever."*

Tom: "*First, let me ask you this: if you knew all that information could you make a better proposal?*"

John: "*I guess so.*"

Tom: "*Then don't you think you need to get it?*"

John: "*Ummmm…*"

Tom: "*And let me ask you two other questions: Does the customer like and / or respect you? And all things being equal, would they prefer to buy from you more than from someone else?*"

John: "*I don't know.*"

Tom: "*Don't you think you should at least have a good idea?*"

John: "*Okay, so what do I need to do?*"

Tom: "*John, for starters you need to do two things. First I need you to have the mindset that I described in Chapter 1 – that every customer is different and has distinct needs, and it's your job to uncover those needs. Second, I need you to see the selling process as an inverted triangle.*"

THE T.R.U.S.T.® TRIANGLE VIEW OF THE SELLING PROCESS

Our friend John is an honest, hard working guy but not among the top sellers. If he has a nice natural personality, and if his company has a solid reputation, he probably will close about 30% to 40% of the proposals he makes. But top sellers can close 70% to 80%, and their close ratio can actually continue to climb throughout their careers as the percentage of their business that comes from referrals continues to grow. These top sellers can literally be two or three times as effective as an average seller like him.

After many years of observation, I'm convinced that the two most critical differences between average sellers like John and top sellers are the two that I told him about in my little coaching session above.

First, the top sellers have a customer mindset. They know that they are not there to deal with a building. They are there to deal with a person! They are there to understand what that person, the customer, wants, and to give the customer just that – what the customer wants. They know that every customer is different, so theoretically every proposal they make could be different as well.

And second, they apply the T.R.U.S.T.® selling process. Let me repeat the three parts of the sales process:

1. Understand what the customer's needs are.
2. Create appropriate solutions to those needs.
3. Show choices and gain agreement to take action – to close the deal.

I often teach selling using the term 'approach' for the first phase where I define the approach as everything that happens between the time you say hello and the time you show the customer what you propose. This way it's clear that the approach also includes introductions, first impressions, and creating interest, in addition to gathering information on customer needs.

When I developed the **T.R.U.S.T.®** model a few years ago I realized there was a better way to talk about these three phases – using the language of the T.R.U.S.T.® model. In T.R.U.S.T.® selling, we do these things:

- We consciously build a **R**elationship with the customer.
- We develop an **U**nderstanding of the customer and his needs so we can create appropriate choices for the customer to consider.
- We **S**how the customer the choices that are available that will satisfy those needs.
- We **T**ake action to help the customer gain the benefits of our products and services.
- We do all of these things under the broad banner of **T**ruth – honesty in all aspects of the interaction.

So now the selling process becomes:

- Build a customer **R**elationship and **U**nderstand the customer's needs.
- Create appropriate choices.
- **S**how how we propose to satisfy those needs.
- **T**ake action to move ahead.

Let's go back to our sales guy, John. How long did John spend building a **R**elationship and **U**nderstanding the specific needs of Mr. Jones? It was actually just the few seconds that he took to introduce himself before moving on to his job survey.

After his survey he moved on to **S**howing the customer his proposal, which would also take just a few minutes.

If we had kept the scenario going and watched him go to the **T**ake action phase, how long might that phase have taken? Well, it could be a long time if the customer starts asking questions and raising objections like:

- *"Why does it cost so much? Your competitor was $300 lower."*
- *"Is this the only model you have?"*
- *"My brother-in-law told me his unit has a lifetime guarantee. Does this one?"*
- *"I've been reading about various other brands on the internet and this one didn't get the top rating."*
- *"Will it be as noisy as my old one?"*
- *"Will it prevent the cold drafts we get now?"*
- *"Why did your competitor include a new thermostat and you didn't?"*

When an in-home salesperson does not get the order is it because they did not close effectively? Or is it because they did not do an effective job of showing their proposal? It's more likely that their failure to get the order is a result of not building an effective relationship and not doing an effective job of understanding the customer's needs. Not closing a sale is more often related to what didn't happen in phase 1 in the selling process than it is to what did happen in phase 2 or phase 3!

So today the typical sales call for the average salesperson looks like this:

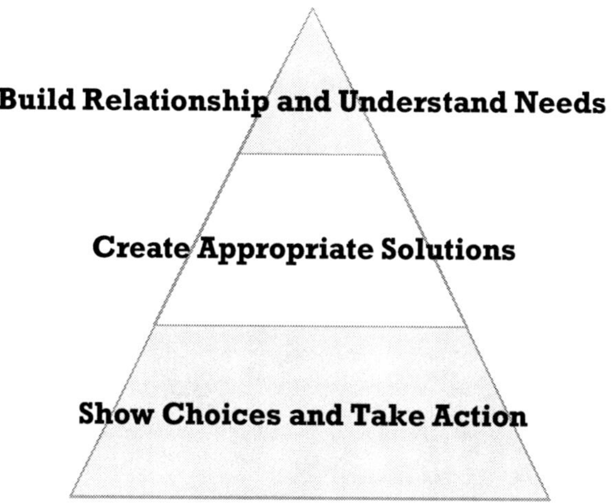

Phase 1, which includes building a relationship and understanding the customer's needs, is typically the **shortest** phase!

For the best salespersons the typical sales call looks like this:

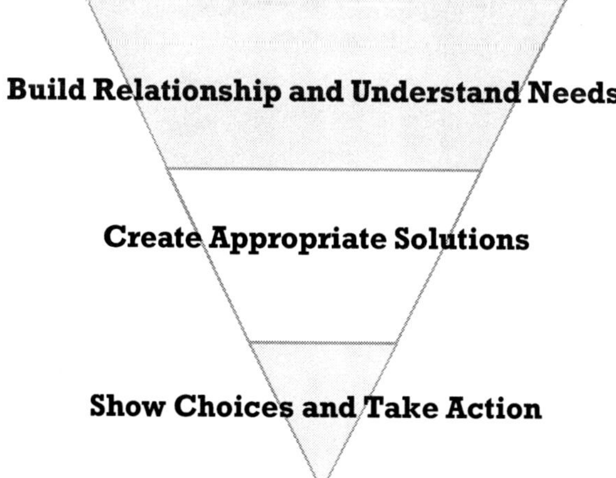

Now phase 1 is the longest phase! Here is why the first phase of the selling process must be the longest phase. In phase 1 we need to:

- Build a **R**elationship with the customer.
- Get a clear **U**nderstanding of the customer's needs.

How do you build a relationship with another person? By talking to and listening to that person! That simply takes time!

How do you get an understanding of where another person is coming from? By talking to and listening to that person! That simply takes time!

I already described the link between the understanding phase of the process and the relationship phase of the process. I pointed out that they form a closed loop. The very act of trying to understand the customer's needs by asking questions and listening is what builds the relationship. And as the relationship builds, we gain a deeper understanding of the customer, which deepens the relationship.

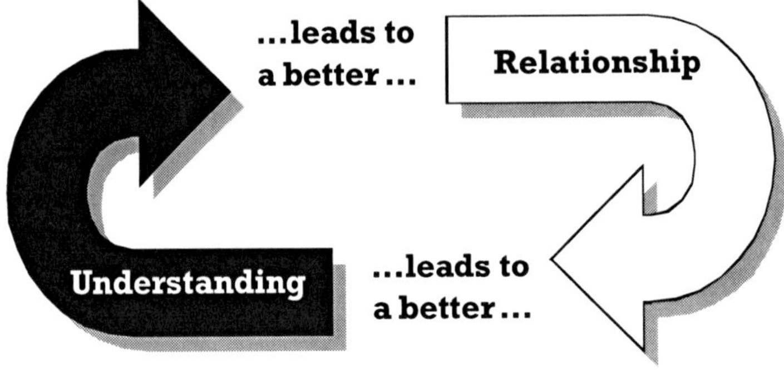

Remember, it's a **loop**!

Most of us like to talk with other people. We like to share our experiences and hear about their experiences. Since this can be the most enjoyable part of the entire sales process, it took me a long time to understand why so many salespeople just plain skip it!

I got the answer to that question a number of years ago when I started teaching in-home salespeople how to sell heating and air-conditioning systems using a process we called 'system selling.' Every heating and air-conditioning manufacturer offers a huge variety of models, and the industry offers a huge number of accessory products – zoning, filters, ventilation, safety and health related products. The upshot is that there are almost an infinite number of possible system combinations.

You simply cannot recommend the best choice of solutions without a **customer** oriented survey tool. Nearly every salesperson I observed up to that point used a **job** oriented survey tool – one that focused on equipment size, home construction, home size, etc. Almost no one had a customer oriented survey.

Let me give you one simple example of how important this is. Let's say we have a customer who wants to replace a furnace. Our job survey tells us that the current model is an 80,000 BTU minimum efficiency model. Our job survey also tells us that the unit is correctly sized. So we just quote a replacement 80,000 BTU minimum efficiency replacement furnace, right? But wait… maybe the customer would like to save energy with a more efficient unit. Maybe they'd like a unit that is quieter, or more comfortable. Maybe they'd like certain accessories. We can't know any of that unless we talk to, listen to, and educate the customer on what's available. The key to doing that effectively is by using the customer survey.

Every in-home salesperson should have considered, in advance, the most important questions that need to be answered to have a complete understanding of the customer's needs! Let me repeat this… **you're not there to deal with a building. You're there to deal with a person!**

It doesn't matter if you're selling air-conditioning or replacement windows or kitchen remodels. There are certain things you need to know about the customer before you can make the best recommendation. Some of the questions that get at important customer information apply to virtually every in-home selling situation. Here are six questions that can apply in just about every situation:

1. "*How did you hear about our company?*"

2. *"How long do you plan to live in this home?"*
3. *"Why are you taking action at this particular time?"*
4. *"What have you liked about your current ______?"*
5. *"Are there things that you wish were better with regard to your current ______?"*
6. *"Are there any related areas or problems that you would like us to take a look at?"*

The answers to these six questions, and to the follow-up questions that are naturally going to arise from your dialogue with the customer, are going to provide you with a wealth of information you can use. Here's just some of what you're going to learn:

- Did you get a personal referral?
- Are there any special time requirements?
- Does the customer have reasonable installation time expectations?
- Does a pay back story make sense?
- Does a higher quality / longer warranty solution make sense?
- How knowledgeable is the customer on what's available to them?
- What features / benefits do you need to retain?
- What features / benefits could you possibly add?
- Are you the only bidder?
- How else could you help this customer?

In addition to the six basic questions, you need to also think about questions that are specific to your product or service. For example, if you are selling heating and air-conditioning, you will want to ask about energy efficiency, health concerns, etc. If you are selling security systems, you will want to not only ask about safety concerns and lifestyle issues, but possibly about related areas such as fire protection, CO2 monitoring, temperature or flood monitoring.

A WRITTEN CUSTOMER SURVEY IS KEY

I've taught thousands of in-home sales people the value of a customer oriented survey. My best guess is that maybe 1 out of 20 actually goes home, takes the time to put this together, gets the surveys printed, and uses one on each sales opportunity.

By the way, my other best guess is that the 5% who do this are significantly more successful, and better paid than those who don't use a written survey.

Here are the reasons some give on why they might not use a written customer survey:

- They don't have the time to get it done.
- They think they'll remember to ask the questions without having to write them out.

Here are the reasons to use a written customer survey:

- The mere presence of a customer survey conveys the message to the customer that you are organized, professional, serious, interested in them as an individual, and different from your competitor.
- The presence of a customer survey tells the customer that they need to be prepared to spend some time with you.
- A survey virtually guarantees that you will not skip over phase 1 – the relationship and understanding phase.
- You won't miss any areas, because they are written down.
- A survey is a listening tool, not a talking tool. You ask the question and listen to and write down the answers. (More on this later!)
- The survey questions will lead to opportunities to educate the

customer. For example, if you ask how long the customer plans to remain in the home, the answer may start with, "Why is that important?" You now have the opportunity to educate the customer on issues of product quality and economic pay back.

- You'll close more sales, sell more and make more money!

Why would you possibly not do that?

In later chapters, we'll give you some hints on customer surveys and how to make them more effective. For now let me just end with the point that a customer survey can be your very best tool when it comes to inverting your sales triangle.

THE T.R.U.S.T.® SELLING PROCESS

Now that you have an understanding of what your sales call should include and how it should progress from beginning to end, let's put it all together in a way that you'll easily remember while you're in the home. Here's our inverted triangle with easier to remember steps:

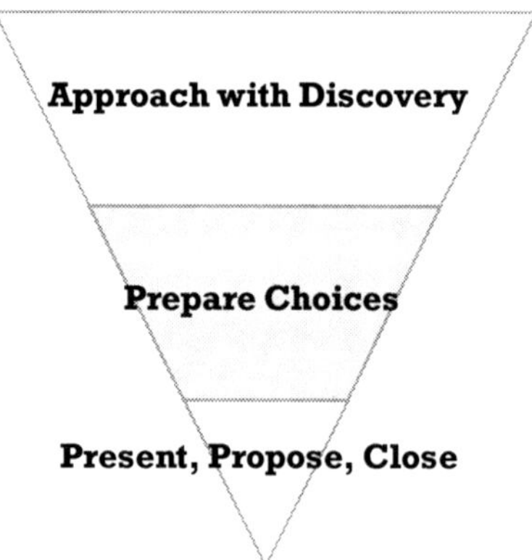

Approach with Discovery includes everything you need to do from the first moment of customer contact – confirming the appointment, showing up on time, your personal appearance, how you meet and greet, your walk-through, taking measurements, using the customer survey, and looking at the existing equipment or products. Everything you do here is intended to create an effective relationship and to discover what is most important to your customer.

Preparing Choices includes all those things you do at the kitchen table when preparing solutions for your customer to consider. This may include sizing, designing, estimating energy savings, and certainly writing your proposal.

Present, Propose and Close is showtime! This should be the easiest and most enjoyable part of the call. Here you're simply affirming what your customer had said was important, gaining agreement that those things are important, presenting your company's important attributes, presenting your recommended solutions as 'choices' for the customer to pick from, and confidently asking for the sale.

As we transition now to a series of chapters that cover the key skills that in-home sellers need to have, I want to leave you with a one-page summary of the first three chapters, a summary that I hope will help you to see THE BIG PICTURE. This summary is also repeated in the appendix at the back of this book so that you can tear it out if you like and keep it in your vehicle. Look at it before you knock on the door on each call.

With the right MINDSET, the right GOALS, and the right VISION of the selling process, you'll already be more than halfway there to a successful sale.

THE BIG PICTURE

MY MINDSET

1. Every customer is a unique individual with different needs / wants.
2. My job is to understand each customer so that I can propose solutions that best fit their needs / wants.
3. When my customers choose me and my company they will get a great value for their investment and be very happy that they chose us.

MY GOAL FOR EACH CALL

1. Gain customer agreement to take action by proposing the best solution for that customer.
2. Achieve a level of customer satisfaction that will cause this customer to call me again in the future and to refer other customers to me.

SELLING WITH T.R.U.S.T.®

T Truth – honesty in all aspects of the sale

R Create a **Relationship**

U Understand the customer's needs / wants

S Show the customer choices

T Take action

THE T.R.U.S.T.® SELLING PROCESS

1. Approach with Discovery
2. Prepare Choices
3. Present
4. Propose
5. Close

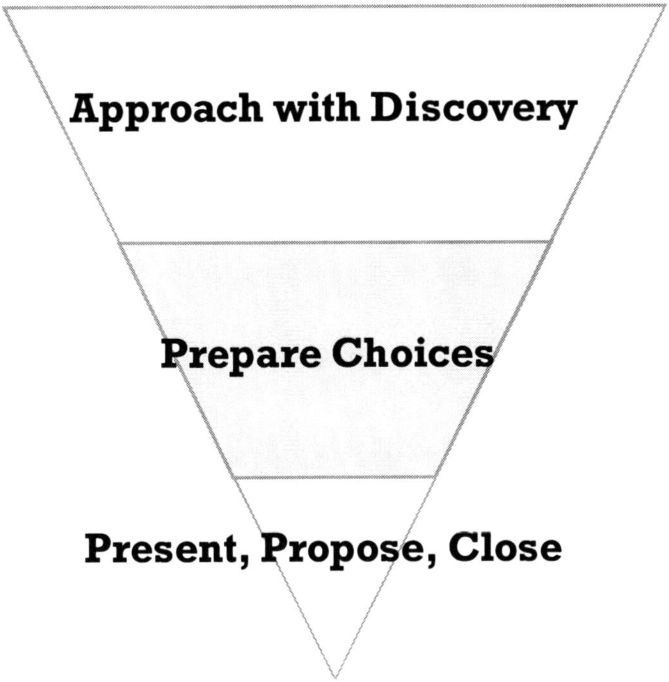

Approach with Discovery

Prepare Choices

Present, Propose, Close

CHAPTER 4

A Checklist For Success: Breaking T.R.U.S.T.® Selling Into 10 Steps

If you're still with me, you should understand the T.R.U.S.T.® selling process. T.R.U.S.T.® is real selling – no gimmicks – just sound, basic selling. In T.R.U.S.T.® selling we have two goals.

First, **find out what this particular customer wants** and **help him or her to get it.**

And second, **leave the customer so satisfied that he or she will call you again in the future, and will refer other people to you.**

This chapter converts that simple sales process to a series of 10 steps and offers a basic checklist to follow. These ten steps are repeated on a single page in the appendix. I suggest that when you complete this book you tear out that page and keep it where you will look at it frequently. A pilot with 40 years of flying experience wouldn't think of taking off without going through the pre-flight checklist. You can use this method, too. Don't start a sale without reviewing the 'pre-flight checklist.'

THE 10-STEP T.R.U.S.T.® IN-HOME SALES PROCESS

I know 10 steps sounds like a lot to remember. Sorry about that, but I never said becoming a truly professional salesperson was going to be easy. Actually it's not as bad as it sounds. The 10 steps include things you do before you even see the customer, the things you do during the call, and the things you do after the call.

Here are the 10 steps lined up with the T.R.U.S.T.® In-Home Selling Process:

Approach with Discovery

Step 1 Prepare mentally; have the right mindset.

Step 2 Gather and organize company and supplier material.

Step 3 Check your appearance and focus.

Step 4 Greet the customer and make a strong first impression.

Step 5 Discover the customer's wants and needs, and complete any required physical survey of the job.

Prepare Choices

Step 6 Prepare your proposal.

Present, Propose and Close

Step 7 Present the proposal.

Step 8 Ask for the order and respond to questions or objections.

Step 9 Make the sale and give reassurance.

Step 10 Take 'customer-for-life' actions.

In the rest of this chapter I'm going to discuss each step in detail. There are a number of underlying skills, such as benefit selling, closing, and objection handling, that I will mention in some of the steps. The skills themselves will be covered in detail in later chapters.

STEP 1 - PREPARE MENTALLY; HAVE THE RIGHT MINDSET.

When you are ready to deal with a potential customer, you have to make a decision on how you are going to think about that person. Our culture tends to force everyone into groups – rich, middle class, poor, suburbanites, exurbanites, older folks, yuppies, woofs ('well off old folks'), etc. The fact is that while these labels might apply in a generic way, they have nothing to do with individual people. Two homeowners living side-by-side in the same neighborhood in nearly identical homes can be as different as night and day. If you treat them as if they are simply part of the same group or type, you're going to be off the mark most of the time.

So before you engage any new customer contact, repeat to yourself, "*This customer is unique. I do not know his or her specific needs and desires, nor do I know his or her personal style. It is my job to uncover this knowledge so that I can gain his or her confidence and respect and so that I can make the best possible proposal and earn the sale.*"

That's your job in step one. You must get your head into this individual customer!

STEP 2 - GATHER AND ORGANIZE COMPANY AND SUPPLIER MATERIAL.

You know that you are a professional. You are competent, well-trained, and fully capable of doing a good job for your customer. But your customers don't know that. They will judge you, and they will decide if you are a salesperson that they like, respect, and want to do business with. The way you are organized will send an important message.

I personally do not believe you should make an in-home sales call without at least one professional looking sales binder and possibly as many as three separate binders.

Hold on! Before some of you techies start yelling, I know that some of you think that 'binders' are old-fashioned, and I do not disagree. So feel free to substitute 'laptop-based package' for 'binder' if you wish. I think you will see that a good old-fashioned physical three-ring binder is still good for some things that might be hard to do with a laptop, but please read on. If you have the computer skills to replicate the tools I'm going to discuss, that's great!

First, you need a complete set of company and / or supplier brochures and support tools. Customers will ask you questions. You want to be able to simply open a binder (or go to a computer file) and pull up the answer. Also remember that people learn better visually. Sometimes a picture or diagram in a brochure can explain something better than a lot of confusing words. And remember that people like to see things in print. It's one thing to say to a customer, "*The XYZ model is 30% more efficient so it can save an average homeowner more than $300 per year,*" and it's another thing to show that in a brochure that has actual supporting savings charts, calculation tools, and third party certification. It just adds to your credibility.

So, you need to be able to reach for or access any information you need. For many sales folks, good old three-ring binders with tabs will get this job done. In some cases there might be so much material that the binder can become a sales sample case. The point is you need all your company and supplier tools at your fingertips.

Second, you need an 'evidence' binder that proves your company's capabilities. It should have pictures of your company's work. The best ones have captions and explain to the customer what they are looking at. In other words, if you sell air-conditioning, a picture of a run of duct work doesn't mean much to most people. But if it's appropriately captioned with remarks such as, "*We cross break square ducts to eliminate expansion noise*" or "*We tape all joints to eliminate expensive air leakage,*" most homeowners will get the point that you do a top quality job.

Your evidence binder should also include recently written customer testimonial letters from satisfied customers.

And third, your evidence binder can have copies of any recognition awards, or trade association memberships or anything that helps prove the point that your company is a top service provider.

You can use this binder very effectively by leaving it with the customers while you are working on your proposal after the discovery portion of your call is complete. Once you have completed your job survey and your customer survey you'll need time to put together your proposal. You can maximize the use of that time with the evidence binder. Like this:

"*Mr. and Mrs. Smith, I think I have all the information I need to put together a proposal for you. This usually takes me about a half hour. Here is a binder that you might like to flip through that will give you an idea of the kind of work we have done for other folks, and also there are some nice thank you letters from satisfied customers that you can glance at. Okay? Any final questions that you have before I put together the proposal?*"

The third binder, and the most important one, is your professional presentation binder. Your goal is to close this sale. It simply makes sense to do everything you can to maximize the chances of that happening. We have learned, through years of experience, that the best way to add value to your offering is to walk the customer through a fairly brief (less than 10 minutes), but thorough, company presentation **before** presenting the proposal.

For this presentation to be made in the most professional manner you must have a professional presentation binder or laptop presentation.

The other tool you need to prepare before your call is your customer survey form.

In the last chapter we ran through a list of questions that could be asked on just about any in-home sales call, for example:

- *"How did you hear about our company?"*
- *"What prompted you to call us at this particular time?"*
- *"In general terms, what are some of your most important considerations in buying this new product?"*
- *"Do you know how long you might be planning to live in this home?"*
- *"How do you like your current product?"*
- *"What would you like to see improved in your current product?"*

Equally important, you want to ask questions related to your specific offering. For example, if you sell heating and air-conditioning, you might ask a series of questions regarding energy cost concerns, comfort concerns, noise issues, even health issues. If you sell replacement windows you might focus more on aesthetic preferences, materials, energy costs, or security levels desired.

You need to remember that there are a lot of important reasons to ask all these questions.

First, we do want the answers. Answers will tell us what this particular customer needs or wants from a supplier.

Second, asking these questions communicates instantly to the customer that you do, in fact, want to understand him or her. You care enough about the customer to take the time to ask questions, to listen carefully to the response, and to write down his or her response.

The third reason is this. Asking questions begins dialogue. Dialogue helps establish rapport, and rapport leads to a relationship with the customer. As you talk with one another you cease to be strangers. You become consultant and client. You may even become friends.

Again, based on my years of personal experience, the best way to ensure that the questions get asked (so that these three results can occur) is to use a printed survey form.

A printed form does a lot of things. It assures that you'll ask all of the questions. It puts the customer at ease. They can see that you're not just being nosey; you're trying to gather the information you need to make a better, more customized proposal. It gives you a place to write down the customer's responses. This gives visual feedback to the customer that their answer is important because you wrote it down after all!

A written form also gives you a place to record the answer to what I call 'importance ranking' questions. These ranking questions really give you absolute feedback on what to include in your proposal. Let me give you one example using our heating and air-conditioning salesperson as a model.

We ask a question or two during the home survey about energy usage. For example, we might ask, "*How do you feel about your current electricity costs for cooling; are they about right or too high?*" The customer might respond, "*Well, I'd like to see them lower.*" This suggests a more energy efficient system might be appropriate.

Another question that we might have on our survey would be, "*About how long do you plan to live in this house?*" Say the customer responds, "*Oh, at least 10 years.*" Again, this suggests that an energy savings / pay back proposal might make sense for this customer.

Our importance ranking follow-up question can really nail this down for us and for the customer as well. So we ask the question, "*Is this important enough for me to show you some choices on how you can address that concern?*" Another way to put this might be, "*Would you like me to show you some energy saving options on my proposal?*" The phrasing is not important. Just remember that you are trying to evaluate which information you are getting from the customer is most important so that you can refer to it later... "*You said that cutting your cooling costs was important to you.*"

This is selling at its best. You ask questions, you listen, and you ask follow-up questions. You're getting information. You're showing the customers that you care about their particular needs. You're building a relationship with the customer. That's why you need tools like the survey form so you can drive that **U**nderstanding and **R**elationship loop.

Selling is complex. To sell at a truly professional level requires training, self discipline, an interest in people, mastery of some basic skills (including sales skills), communication skills, planning and problem solving skills, and also organizational skills. I would say that about half of your success depends on what you do in front of the customer, but the other half reflects what you do **before** you make a call. In my career, I had a lot of opportunity to do business-to-business selling, calling on manufacturers, wholesalers, builders and contractors. Possibly because so many of these sales required complicated and lengthy sales cycles, everyone just seemed to accept that you needed PowerPoint presentations, binders, handouts and written proposals – and that all had to be prepared in advance.

I've also had a lot of opportunity to do in-home consumer selling and to observe others doing in-home selling. I'm always surprised at how few in-home sellers are fully and professionally prepared. They just don't take the time to put together the tools to maximize their chances of success.

This is critical folks! You only get one chance. If you'll do this step, you're going to look prepared, organized and professional. In addition, your sales tools will guide your sales process just like a pilot's checklist guides how he lands a 777.

And if you don't do this step, you're going to be unprepared, disorganized, and unprofessional by comparison. Every call will be just a seat-of-the-pants experience.

So enough nagging. Do the necessary preparation work to look and sell like a professional.

STEP 3 - CHECK YOUR APPEARANCE AND YOUR FOCUS.

If you've done steps 1 and 2, and if you've done them conscientiously, you are as ready as you could possibly be to make a professional sales call.

Now just one last thing before you ring the doorbell. Let's make sure you are ready to meet this particular customer and to get to know them well enough to make the perfect proposal.

This is the time to stop, take a deep breath, try to put aside other things on your mind, and bring this sales call up to your number one priority for the next 2 hours.

The impression you make on the customer is going to depend on what you say and how you say it, but it's also going to depend on how you look and act. Put thought and care into your personal appearance and actions.

Does the vehicle that you are about to pull up in front of the customer's home reflect the message you want to send? Is your car or truck neat and clean? Perhaps a hybrid vehicle might convey the message that you are personally committed to helping reduce your carbon footprint.

Are your clothes appropriate? I know it would be silly to suggest that if you've been working on equipment that you're not going to get dirty. It may not be possible to change before you need to make a sales call. People understand that. But clearly, neater is better, because you are going to create an impression whether you want to or not. The rule of thumb would be 'do the best you can.'

I strongly suggest a name badge or photo ID badge of some sort. You are going into a person's home, and she will want to feel confident that you are who you say you are. The best is a photo ID badge with your company name and your name large enough to read from several feet away.

Make a final check of your personal appearance. Comb your hair, check in the mirror, and practice smiling.

Last, focus your attention on the task at hand. Turn off your cell phone. Commit yourself to this call. Look carefully at the home you are about to enter, taking in everything you can. Pay particular attention to anything that you could compliment the homeowner on as part of your greeting. A nice neighborhood? A particularly nice garden? A new car in the drive? A deluxe fishing boat in the garage? You get the point. Start thinking of this customer as an individual.

STEP 4 - GREET THE CUSTOMER AND MAKE A STRONG FIRST IMPRESSION.

I'd like you to treat the greeting as a separate step because it has two unique purposes in the sales process. Specifically, we need to create a strong first impression, and we need to set the customer's expectations for what is going to follow. If we don't accomplish these two goals it's going to make it very difficult to have a successful call.

Obviously you want to make the best possible first impression. Some of this is just common sense: a firm handshake, eye contact, and using the customer's full name until they ask you to be less formal. For example, "*Mr. and Mrs. Smith? I'm Jane Jones from Metro Air-conditioning. I'm very pleased to meet you.*" Also, have business cards ready to hand out and be sure to give cards to both husband and wife if both are present.

A point worth noting here is that in today's world women make the majority of decisions about expenditures that affect the home. Even if you sell a fairly technical product like heating and air-conditioning, the wife will normally have a lot to say about the amount that will be spent. For all you know she might be a mechanical engineer! When you sell to couples in the home you simply do not want to direct all of your attention to either spouse unless it becomes very clear later in the call that one or the other will make the decision.

It is important to show enthusiasm for this call and for meeting these people. You need to demonstrate in every way that you can that this is important to you. This will make the call important to the customers as well.

After you introduce yourself it is often appropriate to use a personal compliment. Many people are proud of their homes, and if that is the case, compliment the home. "*What a beautiful home. I just love the character in these older homes. How long have you lived here?*" It's important to make sure that you are sincere in your compliment. Find something you know and care about.

Once the niceties are out of the way, you want to tell the customer what is going to follow and gain the customer's agreement to participate.

Remember the next step is going to be the actual survey and questioning process to uncover both the **physical** job requirements **and** the specific **needs** of these customers. You need their agreement to participate in that process with you. To gain that agreement you should have a clear, concise 'story' that you use to explain what is going to happen and why. The 'why' is always the same – because it will **benefit** the customer to participate!

Here is an example:

"*I really want to thank you, Mr. and Mrs. Smith, for giving us the opportunity to give you a proposal on your new (system, projects, etc.). I want to be sure that our proposal takes into account any wishes or concerns that either of you might have, so I do have a few questions that I'd like to go over with you. I also need to survey the exact job requirements by looking at your current (system, installation, etc.). What I find most useful, if you have a few minutes, is to have you accompany me while I survey the job, and I'll ask you questions as we go. Is that okay with you folks?*"

Most people will say "*sure,*" especially if this expectation was raised by the person setting your appointments, or by you personally when you confirmed the appointment. If that isn't happening now it's incumbent on you to have it established.

Some customers might have a legitimate reason to leave such as, "*Gee, I need to pick up the kids in 25 minutes, so I need to leave soon.*"

Whatever the situation, be flexible, but be clear. You can come back, call back, or reschedule, whatever. But you need to spend enough time with the customer to get to know them and for them to get to know you. Otherwise you're just a business card and a face in the crowd. Worse, your customers are just going to get an off-the-shelf proposal that doesn't fully reflect their individual situation. So you need to communicate that like this:

"*I completely understand. This is a busy time of day at my house, too, with all the kids' activities. I do need to spend about 20 minutes surveying the job, and I also need about 30 minutes of your time. What's the best way to do that for you folks? Should I come back later this evening or would tomorrow be better?*"

STEP 5 – DISCOVER THE CUSTOMER'S NEEDS AND COMPLETE ANY REQUIRED PHYSICAL SURVEY.

Step 5 is not just a physical job survey. It is a process of discovery of information about the customer and information about the job requirements.

The most important skills you will be using in step 5 are the skills of questioning and listening. I devote a complete chapter – Chapter 5 – to these skills.

Another skill you'll use in step 5 is the use of benefit selling, or translating information about products or services into meaningful benefits for the customer.

In this step you will have the opportunity to educate the customer on things that they may not know but which will help them make a better decision. For example, if you asked the customer, "*How do you feel about the current cost of heating your home?*" the customer's likely response is going to be something other than a simple yes or no. He or she might say something like, "*Our bills have really gone up in the past couple of years. I've thought about a newer, more efficient system, but I guess that would depend on how much it would cost... what are we talking about here?*" And you would then need to spend a few minutes educating the customer on energy savings possibilities before you return to your questioning process. Being skilled at benefit selling means being able to provide useful information to the customer in a way that makes it **meaningful** to him or her.

A not-so-good benefit seller might say something like, "*Our model 1350 is the most efficient model at 95%. It would add about $1,000 to the total system price.*"

A good benefit seller might say something like, "*We have models that convert up to 95% of the gas you burn into heat. That compares to only 80% on the least efficient models, so you're reducing fuel use by about 15%. I'd be happy to do an exact calculation, but based on a home of this size I think you'd have a pay back of less than three years. That would be like investing your money in a guaranteed savings account at more than 30% interest. Would you like me to look at that as part of my proposal?*"

Because benefit selling is such a key skill I've also included an entire chapter on that as well in Chapter 6.

Okay, so we're ready to start our survey process. Do these two things right away.

First, ask open questions to get the customer talking. You want them to understand right away that you are the listener and you want them to do the talking. A good question to open with in just about any situation is, "*Could you tell me a little about why you are planning to get a new (system / equipment / etc.) right now?*"

Second, get the customer involved – physically if possible. "*I want to get a quick measurement on the square footage you've got here – could you hold this measuring tape on this corner for me?*"

The more levels on which you can involve the customers, the more likely the customers are to become personally committed to the solution that both you and they are putting together. At the end of this step you would like to be able to sincerely close with a statement like this, "*I certainly appreciate the information you've given me. I think I have a really* *good **understanding** of what you're looking for."*

The customer survey form is another way of involving the customer. You and the customer are working together to develop a complete picture of the job requirements so that the customer can get what he or she really wants! The survey form guides and facilitates the process in several ways:

- You won't miss any important questions – they are written out for you.
- The form acts as a constant reminder that you are supposed to be the questioner / listener and not the talker.
- The presence of the survey form shows the customer that this is a custom proposal – not an off-the-shelf bid.
- The presence of the survey form shows the customer that they do need to participate. You've both got a job to do. It's necessary to collect all of this information so that the customer can get a great proposal that will give them what they need.
- The form provides a place for you to write down the customer's responses to your questions. If the customer's input is truly important, then it is important enough for you to write down!

So in summary, here is how I like to see step 5 progress. You get the customer to accompany you as you survey the job. You ask your survey questions as you go. As the customer asks follow-up questions, you educate them on the benefits that are available to them. You take measurements or collect any other data as you go. Along the way you continually ask the customer if those topics you're discussing are important enough for **you to show them some choices to consider**. These questions give you a clear understanding of what the customer is thinking, and they get the customer committed to what they now expect will be reflected in your proposal.

What if you <u>don't</u> have a customer survey form?

Well, I'm not naïve. I know that despite my pleading, some of you are not going to get around to preparing your formal customer survey form. Bummer. I'll get over it. I'm guessing you were almost done with that when the dog ate it. So now you have to proceed without it. Here are a few thoughts just in case.

I'm assuming you still have a job survey form of some kind that gives you a place to record measurements, note equipment model numbers, etc. One thing you could do is at least jot a few key phrases down on the back of your form to remind you that you do need to ask for customer input. These could be words or phrases like customer key goals, energy concerns, likes and dislikes regarding current system, and most important – benefits desired.

You could also keep a notebook like engineers use to record customer input. If you'll at least do something like the above, you'll have a piece of paper and a pen in your hand that will remind you that you're supposed to be talking to the customer.

How long can Step 5 last?

Some heating and air-conditioning sales people arrive at a home, do a quick survey, prepare a generic proposal, give it to the customers, and are back on the road in less than 30 minutes. These sales people typically bid a basic, no-frills system and they have low close rates, as you would expect.

I also know heating and air-conditioning sales people who spend two hours with the customer just in the discovery phase. They quote customized systems that have significant enhancement content and include add-ons such as maintenance agreements and extended warranties. They have high close ratios and high average dollars per sale… and high incomes.

I can't tell you exactly how long you should take with step 5 because it's going to vary depending on your product line. But I can tell you this, you can safely keep talking with the customer as long as he or she is engaged and interested in what you are discussing.

Sometimes sales people will say they just can't afford to spend the kind of time I am talking about here. My answer would be that if you can double your close rate, and you can double your average sale, you could easily justify spending four times the amount of time that you now spend on each sale!

You need to do your own numbers. Just remember that the more time and effort you put into step 5, the better your chances are of closing the sale; the better your chances are of selling a higher featured job; and the better your chances are of getting a future referral – and what's the value of that?

STEP 6 - PREPARE YOUR PROPOSAL.

Now you have all the information you need to put together a compelling proposal for the customer.

In most cases I like to see a salesperson complete his or her proposal right where the customer can see what that process entails. Usually, this is the kitchen table. Assuming that you are well prepared it will allow the customer to observe your professionalism. It also communicates the timeframe that the customer can expect so that they stay involved in the process.

Here is some phrasing that I suggest, "*I really appreciate your spending this time with me. I think I have a good understanding of all the job requirements. Now, I need just about 30 minutes to put all this material together in a proposal for you, and then I'd like to go over it with you this evening. Do you have a place I can work for a few minutes maybe right here at the kitchen table? Before I begin that, do you have any final questions or comments you'd like to add?*"

If you have an 'evidence binder' – this is the time to use that. "*Here's a binder with photos of some of our work and letters from some of our satisfied customers. You're more than welcome to flip through that while I'm putting this together.*"

Obviously there are some sales situations where the proposal simply can't be put together in the home due to the fact that drawings or other technical elements need to be added. In this case, I still like the idea of leaving an evidence binder behind. I also suggest that you should try to use the same kind of wording that I used above to be sure the customer is committed to the next step. It is particularly important that all the buyers be there when you review your proposal.

"It will take me a day to get the final proposal put together for you folks. I'd like to come back about the same time tomorrow evening if both of you can be available at that time. If that's okay, I'll also leave this binder here for you to look at if you have a chance. It's got some very good pictures of our work on other jobs and also some nice letters from other folks that we have done work for. Okay?"

One proposal... or multiple choices?

I started teaching in-home sales people in 1994, so it's been almost 15 years that I've been grappling with the best way to structure a proposal for the homeowner. There are two basic possibilities. You can just propose a single solution, or you can propose a choice of solutions: a best-better-good choice.

The latter is hands-down the most effective way to sell. In just about every case, we should give the homeowner a choice.

Some sales people only quote the cheapest, most stripped-down solution that they have. Why do they do that? I guess it's because they simply believe that all people want is a cheap solution, and they know that 'Joe the price cutter' is probably going to be bidding. So their thinking goes like this, "*People want a low price, and they will think I'm trying to cheat them if I come in too high. I think Joe the price cutter is going to be around $4,000. We do better work than Joe, so I think I can ask for a 5% premium. So I'll bid $4,200 for a low-end solution.*"

Wow! Look at the erroneous thinking here.

In the first place, we're not 'bidding.' We are proposing a sound solution to the customer's requirements.

Second, it's not true that all people want is low price. If that were true you'd never see another Lexus, another Polo shirt, or another muffin at Starbucks. What people do want is what they believe is a good value for them. We know from basic consumer research (the research I referred to in Chapter 1) that if customers are offered a low-priced product, a medium-featured product, and a deluxe-featured product, about **half** will take the medium-featured, and a quarter will take the deluxe-featured. Only 25% will opt for the lowest price if they are given valid choices.

If you've read the first three chapters, I don't know how you could ever just bid the cheapest job you can.

That still leaves us, however, with two valid options when it comes to our proposal. We could offer a single solution or we could offer a choice of solutions. Some people would say that if you have spent a significant amount of time with the homeowners and have done a really good job developing a clear understanding of their needs, that you could just propose the one solution that best fits those needs.

I am personally confident – after I've spent a long time talking with any customer – that I know which solution best fits the customer's requirements. So why not just propose that solution?

Because when a customer is buying in a retail environment, they are already pre-conditioned when it comes to price. For example, if I decide I want to buy a Polo shirt for $50, I do that already knowing that I could buy the store's private label brand for $25. The prices are posted for me to see. I've looked at the sales flyers that come with the Sunday paper. I've gone online to check prices. Retail customers know what consumer items cost.

But most people have no idea what to expect when they call an in-home salesperson. The person on the street could not guess within thousands of dollars what it might cost to re-roof a house, replace a furnace, or put new windows in a home.

The only way I can see to deal with this issue is to propose multiple solutions. From my direct experience consulting with large contractors,

I know that when salespeople use a best-better-good proposal form, both the dollars per sale and the close rate increase. I think the reasons for this are probably obvious, but here they are anyway.

First, if I show a value proposal in addition to the proposal that I would like to close, then the customer can be confident in my competitiveness. I want the customer to have the 'better' system. But on an apples-to-apples comparison, the customer can see that I am in line with other suppliers.

Second, if I show a 'deluxe' solution in addition to a 'value' or 'better' solution, it allows the customer to put the pricing in perspective. It's a lot easier to justify $30,000 for a new car knowing that I could be paying $45,000. And for the person who actually wants the $45,000 car, there is real satisfaction in knowing just how much better their purchase is than the guy down the block who could only afford the value model. In the same way, it's easier to justify a $12,000 home improvement if I can see that the more deluxe system would actually cost $15,000.

In summary, buyers need to see the total range of both prices and benefits available in order to either justify, or to feel good, about their purchases. The best way for the in-home seller to do that is by showing choices.

I do want to clarify that I am not abdicating my responsibility to fully understand the customer's requirements or to propose the best solution to those requirements. I am not suggesting that we simply offer multiple choices by saying, "*Here's a best, better, and good solution… take your pick.*" On the contrary, I am saying that you should propose the best solution for the customer, but include the others to help the customer evaluate your proposal. For example, "*Here is the solution that I think best fits your requirement. We could look at these other solutions; however, this is the one I think is the best in this situation. May I explain that one first and then we can look at the others if you would like to?*" You will always get a yes to that!

What's included in the presentation package?

Assuming that you are well prepared, you will have your presentation package about three-fourths complete. You have four jobs left:

1. Complete any required or collateral information worksheets that you will need. These could include energy savings and pay back analyses, system or equipment sizing calculations, product layout, etc.

2. Pick the equipment or the choice of products that you are going to propose.

3. Calculate the costs and pricing for each choice and put that onto your proposal document.

4. I almost always recommend a 'choice of financing' close, so calculate the monthly cost for each choice and include that on your proposal.

Here's what a completed presentation package might look like in detail.

1. A company brochure or company capabilities book.

I like to see companies have a printed four-color capabilities brochure or at least a neatly typed capabilities page. I remain convinced that an old fashioned company presentation book is still the most effective way to quickly build value around your company. At a minimum, it should include your mission statement (which stresses customer satisfaction) and a list of key points, such as the number of years you have been in business, professional associations, community activities, and personal certifications achieved. Basically you want to support your contention that you're a highly professional, customer focused organization, and a good citizen whom the customer can trust.

I recommend that you include several photos – maybe two pages with three photos per page. I like to use a photo of the business headquarters (be sure to line up all the company vehicles out front as well) and a photo of the company team. If you have installer teams, take a photo of them. It really helps to personalize the presentation when you can point to this photo and say, "*This is Joe and Fred, – they'll actually be installing your new system for you.*" A few pictures that illustrate the excellent quality of your company's workmanship could also be included.

Make copies of any documents that show you are fully in compliance with all rules and regulations, such as a business or contractor's license, or your liability insurance policy. Remember, even if some of these documents are required for all companies, only those who remember to show them to the customer get credit for having them. Put these in plastic sleeve pages and include them in the binder.

Include any documents that show that all companies and all jobs are not created equal. In my HVAC contractor seminars I supply my students with two tools that fit here. The first is a collection of facts related to HVAC installations, such as the fact that 90% of all systems are installed with some kind of energy wasting error. These facts show that two companies can install the exact same equipment and end up with two different results. I'm sure you can find something similar for your product lines. Trade associations are a good source for that kind of information.

The second tool is a graphic of an iceberg. I love this graphic! It shows that 90% of an iceberg is below the surface – illustrating that good installation and sound business practices are not always visible to the customer. But, they are actually the most important part of the job! If you e-mail me I'll send you a copy of this graphic. Then I recommend that you show right on the graphic the things that the customer can see – the physical equipment that you sell. And below the surface show the things that the customers can't see – training, years of experience, best practices, employee policies, and warranties.

2. Brochures on the equipment you have selected for the customer.

You should carry with you clean copies of the manufacturer's literature on all of the possible equipment and accessories you might include on a proposal. Based on what your customer indicated was important to him, select the equipment and accessories you recommend and insert copies of the literature into your binder.

3. Backup calculations.

The most common backup calculation would be on energy savings. If your product saves energy, you want to show exactly how much energy in dollars. Illustrate how the product will pay for itself in energy savings over time. Another calculation you might use would be life costing. This might show the difference between the annual life cost of a 30-year installation and a 40-year installation. In addition, you can show the amount of money the customer will avoid in service costs with longer warranties versus shorter warranties.

4. The proposal worksheet.

Yes, I said 'worksheet.' With a rare exception the typical contractor bid, estimate or quote form is a blend of technical jargon, legalese and details that are of interest to the company but have no value to the customer. In fact all of this is distracting. After years of frustration at trying to get contractors to change their proposal forms to something with a value-added, customer friendly format I came across the idea of using a 'proposal worksheet' to present with. Once agreement occurs and the sale is made, then transfer the important information to the actual contract.

This has the added advantages of being something that can be easily created on any computer, modified at will, and marked up at the kitchen table any way you want. I once sat by while a salesperson told the customers he didn't want to go through all the paperwork unless they were absolutely sure they were going to buy. Don't ever let the paperwork get in the way of making a sale! I have shown a copy of a typical worksheet in the appendix.

STEP 7 - PRESENT THE PROPOSAL

You are now fully prepared to present a professional, persuasive proposal. In most cases this step takes only about 15 minutes. Here's the sequence of steps:

1. Arrange the seating so that you and your customers can all see the presentation while you point to specific items as you talk. Make every effort to allow all of your customers to view the presentation together.

2. Review what the customer said was important using your customer survey form summary. Here is one way to approach this.

"*Well, Mr. and Mrs. Smith, I have the proposal that I've put together for you. As you can imagine there are a number of possible equipment combinations, and I've tried to put together the best choices for you based on our discussion. Let me recap the things that you said were most important to you. First, you said that you wanted a system that would last a long time; that you intended to remain in this house for many years. Next, you said...*"

After you complete a brief review of what the customers said they wanted you can end with, "*Does this cover everything that was important to you?*"

3. Now open your company presentation book. You want to use this to build as much value around your company as possible before you show the proposal and prices. With practice you should be able to review your 10-12 page book in under 7 minutes. Segue to it like this:

   "*Before I show you the equipment I am proposing, I'd like to tell you just a little bit about my company. As you can see in our mission statement, we are committed to 100% customer satisfaction. We have been a family owned and operated business for more than 30 years, so you will have the peace of mind of knowing that we will be around for a long time. We stand behind our work on every installation. Do you have any questions about our mission statement?*"

Move through each page this same way. Point to one or two key items. Comment briefly on why these items are important to the customer. Ask if there are any questions. Move on. Continue this until the last page and then say, "*So, should we look at the choices I've prepared for you to consider?*" Trust me, by now they are ready!

During the company presentation you have been doing the talking. As you have been reviewing each segment, you have been taking the time to ask if the customer has any questions, but it's clearly been your show. Your customer can see that the close is approaching and he or she can also see that this is a more complete proposal and probably a more expensive proposal than they likely had originally anticipated.

Give a brief pause before moving on; this allows you to come to a graceful conclusion to your presentation and it gives the customer a chance to get re-involved if he or she wishes.

STEP 8 - ASK FOR THE SALE AND RESPOND TO QUESTIONS OR OBJECTIONS.

Now you can show the proposal form. The customers' attention will go to the pricing line, but refocus them on the top portion of the form where you have entered their name, address, and phone number. Ask if all of that information appears to be correct. If you are presenting a single solution, proceed to go through each item in your proposal. You don't have to expand on anything because you've already done that; however, it is fine to offer a benefit statement for each item. For example, "*As I said, for your heating I have proposed the Binford Model 123. This will give you the quiet operation and energy savings that we talked about.*"

Highlight areas where you include things that other companies might not.

If you are proposing a range of solutions, which is what I suggest, then explain that before you discuss the best choice. For example, "*What I've done is show you three choices, Mr. and Mrs. Smith. This first system is the one I feel best fits your needs as you explained them to me. However, I have included these other choices for you to consider if you are interested. Would it be okay if I explained the best choice first?"*

When you get to the pricing, you should show a bottom-line total investment and also a monthly finance cost. Your closing question now becomes a simple choice close. For example, "*The investment for the system that matches up the best with your needs is $8,577, or if you were to finance, the monthly investment would be $285. Which of those is better for you?"*

You will get one of four responses when you ask your closing question:

1. "*I'll just write a check,*" or "*We'll just use our home equity line to cover it.*"
2. "*We / I'll need some time to think about that.*"
3. "*That's way more than we expected to pay.*"
4. "*That's just more than we can afford.*"
5. "*We want to get another bid.*"

You need to be prepared for these 'no' responses. None of them is a flat 'no.' With the exception of the first one, they are feedback about unresolved concerns. It's your job to probe these concerns, to help the customer work through these concerns, and even offer alternate solutions. The best way to deal with each of these possible responses is covered in detail in Chapter 7.

If you are effectively able to respond to the customer, then your job is to close once again.

"*So, if we take the energy savings that I've gone through away from the monthly costs, then your real monthly out-of-pocket is reduced to $180. Is that affordable? In that case should I go ahead and set up the installation for the middle of next week?"*

You should continue to dialogue and to close until it's clear that you are simply not going to get a firm commitment on this call. If that occurs, it's important not to leave the customer feeling pressured. Attempt to agree on the next step. Let the customers determine the amount of time they need to consider the proposal.

For example, tell them, "*This is a big decision, and I know you want to consider it carefully. What would be an appropriate time for me to get back in touch with you?*"

STEP 9 – ASK IF THERE ARE ANY OTHER WAYS YOU CAN HELP THE CUSTOMER AND GIVE FINAL ASSURANCE.

Step 9 has three parts:

1. Thank the customer for the order.
2. Ask if you can help in any other way.
3. Reassure the customers that they have made a good decision.

Here is one approach:

"*Thank you very much for your business. I'll stay on top of this to be sure the installation goes smoothly. Before I leave, is there any other service that we can help you with? My company does offer a full line of other gas-fired appliances including high efficiency water heaters and emergency generators. Would you like me to provide you with any information on those offerings? If not, thank you again. I know that you will be very happy with the new system and that it will give you many years of excellent performance.*"

Be aware of the two most common mistakes at this point in the sale. First, if you keep talking, you may raise new concerns or doubts in the customer's mind. You got the order, move on! Second, in your exuberance about closing you can fail to identify other opportunities that didn't come up. Remember to make the customer aware of these other offerings you have. Many HVAC dealers also offer water heaters, fireplaces, and gas powered generators. Many siding companies do roofing, window replacement, and waterproofing. You need to mention this! Even if the customer does not need additional services at this time, you want to leave them with that awareness.

STEP 10 - TAKE 'CUSTOMER FOR LIFE' ACTIONS.

Let me take you back to my thoughts about the importance of a proper mindset in selling. I told you that it is absolutely necessary to have a mindset that every customer is an individual. Here's a second mindset I'd like you to develop. Every customer is potentially a customer-for-life. In many areas of business, companies have 'clients' as opposed to 'customers.' Lawyers, consultants, and financial advisors all have clients. The very term suggests a long-term relationship.

I have found that almost all contractors use the term 'customer.' That term implies a buyer-seller relationship where the objective is to get an order. I'd like you to think of your 'customers' as 'clients.' They are not just your immediate customers; they are future customers. Equally important, they are your source for other new customers through referrals.

In the final chapter of this book I talk about the ways that the most successful salespeople **market** themselves to their customer base. Let me just tell you at this point what I believe are the **minimum** requirements for post-call action.

First, you must send a thank you note to each customer. The best way to do this is to keep a supply of stamped, blank thank you cards right in your vehicle. After every call, pull over and write three sentences on the card, address the envelope and put it into the first mailbox you see.

Second, get the customer into your customer data base.

Third, re-contact the customer after the sale. Thank them again, address and answer any questions (and immediately resolve any concerns they might have), ask for a referral, and ask permission to use them as a reference with other customers.

There you have it… the ten-step sales process. Selling is unpredictable. You have no way of knowing how any particular customer interaction is going to end up. But what you do know is this. If I do all ten of these steps, I will have done everything I possibly could to insure a positive outcome… for this call and for future calls. You can't ask more than that.

CHAPTER 5

Listen Up... And Write It Down

Salespeople are professional communicators. That's what we do.

We're hired to communicate information to potential customers in a way that prompts the customer to make a decision to do business with us instead of a competitor.

It sounds simple enough, but it is actually a challenging assignment. How many naturally great communicators do you personally know? I've been in business now for more than 30 years and I can name only a handful who seem to have been born with that gift. No worries though; we can all learn how to communicate effectively.

In my sales manager training program I teach managers that **leadership** is largely an **outcome of communication skills**! People follow leaders because they believe the leader will take them where they want to go. We follow the person that resonates with us as individuals.

If you've ever been in the military, on an athletic team, or just part of a group, you understand this. The leader is not necessarily the most senior, most experienced, or highest paid. A leader is a person whom people choose to follow.

Sometimes that leader uses verbal skills and sometimes it's in the example he or she sets; we know it when we see it.

The most successful salespeople I have ever met are among the best **communicators** I have met. They **reach** the customer. They are so effective that the customer perceives that the salesperson is truly trying to help them find the absolute best solution to their problem, and the customer **wants** to follow that salesperson to that solution.

I've been working on this for three decades and it's still fun to learn new things. I am confident that **all** of us can be more effective communicators, and that will make us more effective as salespeople.

WHAT IS COMMUNICATION?

If I give a speech and you choose to tune me out, am I communicating? How about if I explain something technical, but you don't understand the underlying concepts, am I communicating? How about if I tell you about the outstanding $5,000 investment opportunity, but you don't have $5,000 to invest, is that communicating?

I'm sure all of you are going to agree that **information** is being shared in all of these cases but that no real **communication** is taking place.

For communication to take place we need two things. First, information needs to be shared in writing, verbally or visually. Second, that information must be received by another person's brain where it can be processed, accepted, rejected, used, filed, retained or even eventually forgotten.

Think for a minute about all of the skills that go into being a good communicator. Here's just a partial list:

- Message development
- Writing
- Speaking
- Questioning

- Listening
- Negotiating
- Conflict resolution
- Using nonverbal communications
- Reading nonverbal communications
- Understanding and dealing with individual differences and personal styles

As you can imagine, there are books written on every one of these communication skills. I Googled just one phrase, 'listening skills,' and got 1.8 million returns. There is a lot of information out there. So in this small book that is specifically devoted to in-home selling I'm not going to do justice to every communication skill. So here's what I propose.

I'm going to spend some time talking about the skill I call L/Q/L: Listen-Question-Listen. This is what we do in T.R.U.S.T.® selling. We probe the customer's needs, wants and desires by asking questions; we listen actively to the answers; we ask more questions; we listen actively; and we ask more questions. Listen-Question-Listen.

According to researchers, about 55% of the total information shared between two people is a result of nonverbal body language. About 35% is a result of the tone of voice being used, and only about 10% is a direct result of the words themselves. I don't know if that's exactly true in every situation, but I sure do know that it's important to understand this.

Effective Questions

Why do we ask questions? Most people reply to that question with the obvious: to get answers. I can think of a number of reasons to ask questions aside from simply getting answers.

Let me give you an example of what I mean. Let's take a simple question that I think just about every in-home seller should have on her survey form: "*Could you tell me how long you've lived in this home and how much longer you are thinking you'll be here?*"

It would obviously be helpful for me to know the answer to this question. It will affect how I present my proposal if the homeowner is planning to get the house ready to sell as opposed to staying indefinitely.

Look at what else this question does for me.

First, it immediately makes the homeowners consider why they are making a home improvement. Is it a short-term fix or is it a long-term investment? The question itself communicates instantly to the homeowner that there may be different solutions available depending on the situation and that they shouldn't be expecting me to produce a one-size-fits-all proposal for them.

Second, any question communicates to the homeowner that I now **know** the answer. Regardless of what I propose, the homeowner knows that I do understand something about their specific situation. Think about that. If I **don't** ask any questions then the homeowner knows that my proposal is generic. But if I ask a lot of questions then the homeowner **knows** that my proposal **could** be customized to their needs.

Third, all the questions I might ask are part of creating a **dialogue**, the goal of which is to develop some kind of personal **relationship**. When we first meet someone that we'd like to have a relationship with, what do we do? We ask them questions like where they're from. We're curious about where they come from, but we're really just starting a conversation. "*Oh, you're from Minnesota? I spent some time there. What town did you live in?*" That's how we converse. That's how we get to know one another.

A fourth reason to ask questions is that it can encourage the homeowners to **think about** an issue or to **educate** them about an issue that they may not be aware of. Let me illustrate this with a different question. I'm going to use my heating and air-conditioning example again, but you could think of a similar question for just about any in-home sale. When a customer inquires about heating and air-conditioning, he is normally thinking only about heating and cooling – I need to stay warm, I need to stay cool. But heating and air-conditioning people might also sell safety devices, health related products, hot water products or even fireplaces. A question on the survey form can direct the customer's attention to areas they are not thinking about. One that I have salespeople ask is whether the family suffers from allergies to anything like dust, pollen or animal dander. Maybe the customer has never even considered that the salesperson could do anything about that problem, and asking the question makes the homeowner realize there may be a solution to his long standing problem. If the answer is 'no,' there is no harm done; but if the answer is 'yes,' then we have opened the door to a whole new line of discussion. So we ask questions because:

- We want to get answers.
- We want to change the customer's expectations about dealing with us as a sales professional.
- We want to make the customers aware that we know stuff about them.
- We want to build a relationship through dialogue.
- We want to get the customers to focus on areas that they might not have even been thinking about.

Now take the **reverse** side of this thinking. Just think about what we **don't** accomplish if we choose not to ask questions. We don't get any information; we don't change the customer's expectations about us; we don't make the customer aware that we know things about them; we don't build a relationship; and we don't get the customer thinking about broader solutions. How can we sell anything that way?

ASKING GOOD QUESTIONS

To me, the only real mistake in selling is to not ask questions. There are two kinds of in-home sellers who don't ask questions.

The first one is the salesperson who hasn't internalized the idea that his job is to interact with the customer. I know salespeople who believe their job is to make an accurate physical survey of the job, to calculate an accurate price quote that will deliver the required margin and to hand that quote to the customer. They don't ask questions because they view themselves as 'estimators.' Measure the job, quote the price, and mission accomplished. This is the mindset issue that I talked about in Chapter 1. These people don't take the time to ask questions, or to get to know the customer, because they don't think that's part of their job!

The second kind of in-home salesperson who doesn't ask questions is the 'expert.' This seller perceives his role as an expert educator to the uneducated homeowner. "*I know what is best for you and I am going to explain it to you, so please listen carefully. You need...*"

You are not just an order taker, technician or product expert. You are supposed to be an expert in developing effective relationships with other people so that you can understand what they need, gain their trust and get them to work with you. That's the same thing as saying that you are supposed to be an expert **communicator**.

That's why we ask questions.

Some questions are better than others either because they produce more dialogue or because they do a better job of directing the dialogue into areas that you need to have the customer consider.

Here's how to develop some good questions.

Make a list of the primary benefits that you offer your customers, such as better comfort, reduced noise, not running out of hot water, improved health, freedom from worry, aesthetic value, pride of ownership, increased safety, longer life, improved resale value, financial savings, return on investment or whatever it is that you offer that will have value.

Now develop at least one question that gets at each key benefit that you offer. Try to make your questions open ended so they can create conversation. In other words, try to get the customer to open up. If you offer increased safety, ask "*How do you feel about the safety level offered by your current system?*" You could ask, "*What are your primary safety concerns?*" Simply identify the benefit you want to discuss and get a conversation started to discover how the customer feels about it.

My favorite open ended, conversation starting phrases in selling to homeowners are, "*Can you tell me about...?*" Or, "*How do you feel about...?*" Or, "*Can you tell me a little bit more about that?*"

I wouldn't ask a question like, *"Does your current system work okay?" I'd ask, "Can you tell me about your current system?*" or "*What have you liked about your current system and what would you like to see improved?*"

I don't think the question, "*If I could show you a 20% return on investment with a more energy efficient unit, would that be of interest to you?*" is as good a question as, "*Can you tell me about your feelings on lower initial price versus lower lifetime ownership costs?*" I wouldn't ask, "*Have you decided on what countertop material you prefer?*" I would ask, "*Can you tell me about how you plan to use the kitchen?*"

Obviously there are times when you have to ask more specific questions, but then you can follow-up with a more open discussion. Let me go back to the example I used earlier. You offer 'improved health' as a possible benefit. So you ask the survey question, "*Does anyone in the family have an allergy to particles like dust, pollen, or animal dander?*" If the answer is simply "*yes,*" the follow-up is "*Can you tell me about that?*"

I'm sure you get my point. Any question is better than no question. Any question that gets the customer to open up is better than one that just gets a yes or no response. And, if you do get a yes or no response, you can just ask another more open follow-up question.

LISTENING

Do any of these scenarios sound familiar to you?

You are at a party or in a large group of people talking to someone and while you're talking to that person she starts glancing around the room to see who else is there. Or you're telling someone about your recent vacation and as you are right in the middle of your description, the other person butts in and starts talking about their vacation, as if they were trying to one-up you. Or you ask your spouse a question and you don't get a response. Did she hear you? Is he just ignoring you? You don't know.

These aren't just life's little irritations. These are proof positive that most people, at least at some moments, are just plain lousy listeners. Lousy listeners, by definition, are lousy communicators.

Sales people are professional communicators. They need to be good listeners.

Researchers tell us that we listen at one of three levels. Level 3, which is the lowest level, is non-engaged listening. This is the way we listen to our spouse at the same time we are trying to follow our favorite TV show. It can produce severe disagreements as in, "You never listen to me!" It has no place in selling.

In level 2 we are engaged but only for our own purposes. We are listening at level 2 when we are thinking, "This person is going on and on about their Caribbean cruise, and as soon as they pause I'll jump in and tell them about my trip to Europe." You're listening at level 2 when you're in the sales meeting and you're thinking, "I know how to solve this problem; I'd better jot down a few notes while I'm waiting for them to get to me."

Level 1, the highest level, is **active listening**. The level 1 listener is **engaged** in the discussion, not just listening to what is said, but trying to **understand the meaning** of what is said and actively **encouraging** the other person to continue to speak.

Level 2 listening results in two people talking at or past one another. Level 1 listening results in a meaningful dialogue.

HOW TO LISTEN 'ACTIVELY'

I said that I wasn't going to be able to give you a complete seminar on listening, but I will give you some very specific ideas that you can apply to the in-home selling situation.

1. Start with eye contact. It's hard for the mind to drift when you're focused on the other person's face. Make solid eye contact at the first greeting, when you ask your questions, and when you listen to the customer's response.

2. Use a printed survey form. Does it sound like I'm nagging you on this? Not only does this form force you to ask good questions but it's also a great active listening tool. Have you ever been introduced to someone and immediately forgotten their name? You were listening at level 2, worried about what you were going to say. You need to write the customer's name down on your survey form while they are saying it. Then, even if you do forget it it's right in front of you. In addition, you can't make eye contact all the time. So what do you do to break eye contact while still appearing to be fully engaged? You write things on your survey form. How important is what the customer is saying? It must be pretty darn important... after all you're writing it down!

3. Use follow-up questions, such as:

    - "*Can you tell me about that?*"
    - "*How do you feel about...?*"
    - "*What else have you done along those lines?*"
    - "*And how did that work out for you?*"

4. Use the "*how important is that to you*" approach that I talked about in Chapter 4. It's the key to your being able to honestly say throughout your proposal presentation, "*You said this was very important to you.*" Any time you can refer to what the customer said, that's active listening.

5. Use the formal company presentation book that I detailed in Chapter 4 as well. Once again, it's a tool that guides you to do the right thing. Present each element by making one or two brief points, then make eye contact and ask, "*Have I given you enough information on that?*" Not only are you practicing active listening but you're encouraging the customer to also be an active listener by keeping them engaged.
6. Use positive body language. This deserves a section all to itself!

USING POSITIVE BODY LANGUAGE

I can give you some basic guidelines for using positive body language, but first here's a warning. We all have body language that we consciously control. The problem is that most of our body language is driven by unconscious thoughts and feelings. You can consciously change it, but first you have to become aware of it.

I strongly believe that every salesperson would benefit from some role play training that includes videotaping interactions between you and another person. You have to see yourself to know whether you tap your foot nervously, whether you get too close to people, or stay too far away, whether you look engaged or are too guarded. If you can't get some videotaped training, then at least ask your boss to observe you on a sales call and look specifically at your body language so you can get some feedback.

Here are some common sense ideas for using effective body language:

The three most effective body language tools for active listening are **eye contact, nodding in positive agreement** with the other person, and **taking notes**. All three of these show that you are engaged, that you're paying attention and that you want the other person to continue speaking.

You should establish and maintain optimum distance from the customer. People do not want you to invade their private space, but getting too far away is just as bad. It can make you look aloof and distant.

If you are seated, such as you would be at a kitchen table, lean forward to show interest. Avoid 'closed' gestures such as crossed arms or legs, or turning partly away from the other person. When addressing a couple, any couple, imagine you have a pointer coming out of your chest and direct that to the space between them. Alternate eye contact between the two people.

This might a good time to expand on the idea of note taking as both an active listening and a body language tool. I want you to understand the importance of note taking. That's why I named this chapter "**Listen Up – And Write It Down.**"

When I am with a potential client on the phone, that person doesn't want to hear me tell them why I'm such a great trainer or consultant. They want to know if I can provide value to their business. So I immediately ask questions about them, their business, goals and challenges. And I take notes – even during a phone conversation. If I didn't, I would not remember exactly what was said. More importantly, I take notes because I want the customer to know that my first goal is to understand their situation. I take notes because I want the customer to perceive me as a consultant who is interested in solving their problems. Consultants take notes.

I take notes because it's an active listening tool that keeps the customer talking to me about their company. I take notes because the act itself helps both me and the customer think. Even on the phone, the customer understands that I'm writing down what she says and the short, quiet pauses are just fine. This gives me time to think. Should I ask a follow-up question or do I understand completely? Do I want to change the subject by asking a question about a different area?

Note taking is a logical, and necessary, adjunct to asking questions in a selling situation!

READING THE CUSTOMER'S BODY LANGUAGE

You can easily read your customer's body language simply by observing the same things I just mentioned above.

If the customer is actively engaged, making eye contact, leaning forward, open in his or her gestures – then everything is a go. Proceed.

But, if I was halfway through my proposal and the customer leaned back, arms crossed, and started looking around the room, I'd probably stop. I'd ask directly, "*I'm sensing that you are thinking about something that I've said. Can you share what that might be with me?*"

LISTEN-QUESTION-LISTEN BRINGS IT ALL TOGETHER

The L/Q/L concept is probably one of the most important skills I ever learned in selling. It reminds me that I'm in a conversation and my role is to learn about the customer's needs and wants so I can serve them in the best way possible. Once I have that done I can start thinking about my proposal.

L/Q/L also reminds me that the sequence of events is not one question, one answer, and then I talk. It's ask an open question, listen to their answer, write it down, ask a follow-up question, listen to their answer, write down what they say... until I completely understand the customer's point, until the customer knows that I understand his point, until I am sure that the customer sees me as different from other salespeople, until the customer is comfortably engaged in a two-way dialog with me, and until I have successfully directed the customer's attention to all the areas I recommend they consider.

Then I can go on to proposing a solution to the customer's problem.

CHAPTER 6

Selling Benefits: Sometimes It's Okay To Sound Like You're Selling

A whole bunch of years ago I walked into a high end men's store 'just to look.' I was looking casually at sport coats and the salesperson approached me. I expected him to say, "*May I help you?*" to which I would then have answered, "*No thanks – just looking*" and that would be that.

But instead, he approached me, extended his hand, and said "*Hi, I'm Rich.*" And he shook my hand and gave me a business card. He continued...

"*That's a nice coat you're looking at – that's 100% wool. Do you wear a coat for work every day?*"

"*Sure, I do.*"

"*I'm guessing that you might be in sales yourself.*"

"*Sure, I am.*"

"*I really like to recommend all wool or wool blend suits and coats for my sales professional clients. The reason is that wool is a natural fabric, so it always looks good. And it has a very rich look to it. Do you travel a lot to see clients?*"

"*Sure, I do.*"

"*You can wear a wool coat like this all day in a car or on an airplane and at the end of the day you'll look just as good as you did when you took off. Do you like this pattern, or can I show you a couple of others that would look very good on you?*"

Wow, this guy sounded like he was **SELLING** something! Well, actually he was. It's actually okay sometimes to **sound** like you're selling. That salesperson was using the **language** of benefit selling.

In Chapter 1 we discussed the fact that people buy things to satisfy needs or wants and we need to understand **each** customer's specific needs or wants before we can know the exact answer to the question of why this particular customer will buy. Then, once we have that understanding, the next step is to help the customer understand how a **particular** product or service solution relates to those specific needs.

Our guy Rich, the sport coat salesperson, in a remarkably short time, used questions to determine that I had at least a general need for a sport coat to wear every day and that it had to fit my need to travel. Based on that knowledge he tried to show me the benefits of all wool coats including professional appearance, freedom from wrinkling, etc.

To this day when I'm in a retail selling situation as a customer and the salesperson is consciously using the skills of professional selling, I still smile to myself. I almost want to say "Congratulations on doing what you get paid to do. Keep up the good work!"

While most salespeople have some working knowledge of benefit selling, an awful lot of them don't actually apply that knowledge.

In this chapter, I'm going to give you a very brief overview of the fundamentals of benefit selling, and I'm going to help you understand the assumptions that salespeople make when they don't actively use benefit selling skills. And… you know what they say about assumptions!

BENEFIT SELLING DEFINED

Okay, so what exactly is 'benefit selling?'

People buy things because they need or want something. I need a new roof. I want a new kitchen. I need a new furnace. I want a new perennial garden. I need to cut my monthly energy costs.

Once you know what a particular customer's needs are, then you can show that customer how your product or service satisfies the need.

That brings us to the **language** of sales. In selling language, if a product satisfies a customer's need, we say it provides a **benefit**. A benefit is something about a product or service that does something for a customer, or in other words, it fills a customer's need.

Benefits are supported by characteristics of the product. We call these characteristics the product's **features.** A feature is literally any characteristic of a product or service. Product features are designed to accomplish some purpose. Sales trainers have historically called this purpose a **function**, or sometimes an **advantage**. So we have the common phrases 'feature / function / benefit' or 'feature / advantage / benefit.'

To give a very simple example, a **feature** of a particular air-conditioning unit may be that it has a very high energy efficiency ratio. The **function or advantage** of having a high energy efficiency ratio is to provide the greatest amount of the cooling with the least possible electrical input. But the **benefit** of having a high energy efficiency ratio is that the customers will save money; they will have a lower electrical bill than they would with a comparable unit that has a lower energy efficiency ratio.

Features – and functions or advantages – support benefits. So, in summary:

- **Feature**: A feature is a specific characteristic of a product, service, or capability.

- **Function / Advantage:** The function or advantage of a feature is what it is designed to do, what it does, or how it works.
- **Benefit:** A benefit is what a particular product, service, or capability can offer a specific customer. A benefit is expressed in terms of results that a customer will be able to recognize in his or her world. It answers the question, "*What will this product do for ME?*"

For the most part, there is no need to make a distinction between features and functions or advantages. While the definitions above are fairly straightforward, you would not have to think of very many product characteristics before you would start to find a lot where it is very questionable whether the characteristic is indeed a feature or a function. For example, if we say that a carbon monoxide monitor sounds an audible alarm if it detects a dangerous level of gas, is that a feature, or a function, or an advantage? The point is that it really doesn't matter. What is critical is that we're able to make a clear distinction between features or functions / advantages and product **benefits**. The benefit of the CO monitor alarm is that it increases the customer's safety.

Let me say this as simply as I can. **Anything** you say about a product or service is either going to be a benefit or it's not. If it's not, I really don't care if it's a feature, function or an advantage. All I really need to know is that it's not a benefit. As a salesperson, every time I open my mouth to present my product or service, I can be saying something about the product or I can be saying something about what the product does to help the customer. You might be able to fool me on whether something is a feature, a function, or an advantage. But you can **never** fool me on whether it's a benefit! It either is… or it isn't.

Let me give you an example. A salesperson makes the statement that, "*The central vacuum means you can just plug in the cleaning hose in any room in the house.*" Is this a benefit or not a benefit? I'm going to guess that most of you are thinking 'benefit.' But if I asked you why, would you give me one of the following answers?

- "*Well, that will save time.*"
- "*That would save work.*"
- "*That would be cool. I could brag to my friends.*"
- "*That would improve air quality by keeping the dirt all in one central place.*"

All true, **but that's not what was said**. What was said is that, "*The central vacuum means you can just plug in the cleaning hose in any room in the house.*" Maybe the salesperson **meant** that it saves time, saves work, adds to self esteem, is more healthy – but that's not what was said.

I've actually just demoed the first assumption that salespeople make that prevents them from selling benefits. They **assume** that if they say something about the product, the customer can **figure out** why that's good! We're obviously going to come back to that simple, but critical, point.

A benefit statement is an actual statement of what the product will do for the customer.

If I were a great benefit seller, here is how I could change what was said in our example: "*The central vacuum means you can just plug in the cleaning hose in any room in the house. This can save a lot of work – you don't have to drag the old heavy machine around. It also means you save time. You just unplug, change rooms, plug back in and you're ready to vacuum. I'm sure you can see the potential health benefits of having the actual mechanism in a central location. You don't recirculate dirty air back into the room where your family has to breathe it. A lot of my customers enjoy telling their friends about their central systems. It's really a top-notch product.*"

That's benefit selling.

TRANSITIONING FROM FEATURES TO BENEFITS

A good benefit seller takes any statement about his or her product or service, and then **transitions** from that statement about the product to a statement or series of statements about how it benefits the customer.

This is the **language of selling**. It actually sounds like selling! You should be saying things like:

- *"May I tell you why this is important?"*
- *"This means that you..."*
- *"This gives you the..."*
- *"So you..."*
- *"Here is what this does for you..."*
- *"We want to help you __________, and here is how we do that."*

Sometimes a good benefit seller will start with a benefit and then support the benefit as needed with product statements like this:

"Because energy costs are so high these days, our company does absolutely everything we can to help you save energy and cut your utility bills. Let me show you just a couple of things. First, we tape every joint..."

Good benefit sellers don't talk about product features and functions in isolation. They talk about what the product can do for the customer and they use information about the product to support them.

Why don't sales people sell benefits? They make assumptions; here are two:

Assumption Number 1

A lot of salespeople don't do benefit selling even though they understand what it is. They don't use transition phrases and other techniques – the language of selling – to actually talk about the benefits.

There is a simple explanation for this. Salespeople, like anyone else, make certain assumptions. The most common assumption that in-home salespeople make is that they think if they just point out the features, the customer will know why they're good.

If we make this assumption, then we say, "*The central vacuum system lets you just plug in the cleaning hose in any room in the house.*" We assume that the customer knows that this will save time, save additional work, be more healthful.

Is this a correct assumption to make? Well, that depends on whether the customer really understands enough about the product to make the transition from feature to benefit on his or her own. We really don't know.

Let me give you a few examples to illustrate my point. Here are five feature statements:

1. "*This unit has a complete five-year parts and labor warranty.*"
2. "*These particular cabinets have solid wood doors and frames.*"
3. "*Our standard thermostat automatically lowers the heat at night or when you're at work.*"
4. "*These shingles will withstand winds up to 150 mph.*"
5. "*This model window is available in five different interior finishes.*"

My guess is that just about any homeowner could tell you at least the primary benefit that he or she would get from each of these features, whether that benefit is peace of mind, pride of ownership or energy savings. Here are five more statements:

1. "*This is our 14 SEER model.*"
2. "*This particular window has an inert gas sealed between the glass layers.*"
3. "*The specs on this roof meet the highest standards of the NAHB.*"
4. "*This exchanger will move up to 300 cfm at high speed.*"
5. "*Its noise output is rated at only 72 dB.*"

Most of the products we sell have at least some technical aspects, and most homeowners don't have a clue about SEER, the NAHB, inert gases, cfm, or decibels.

So **assuming** that throwing out the features or functions is enough for the customer to see the benefits is not a completely valid assumption.

In fact, the older I get the more I understand how little people actually know about what we – contractors in general – do! They invite us into their homes, but they don't know if they can trust us to tell them what they need to know to make a good decision. In many cases they suspect we want to sell them only what is best for us, and not necessarily what is best for them. Let me take just one of our simple statements from the list above and **show you how benefit selling can help educate the customer in a way that builds trust** rather than suspicion.

Sales Rep: "*This particular line of cabinets has solid wood doors and frames. There are actually three reasons we make them that way. The first is strength. Solid wood joinery is much stronger than it is in laminated cabinets, so they last longer saving you money on replacements as well as repairs. I know you have kids about the same age as mine and it's not inconceivable, as you know, that some little person might actually hang on one of these doors.*"

Customer: "*That's for sure.*"

Sales Rep: "*The second reason is that solid wood gives a superior appearance. No laminate joints. No exposed edges. They really give the whole room a look of quality that you can be proud of. And third, is resale value. Here's a magazine article that you can have that points out that the kitchen is the number one sales feature when it comes time to sell. Good kitchen design and quality translate to higher resale price. So what's your general thinking?*"

Customer: *"I like the quality and appearance, and our current cabinets have taken a beating as you can see. But I am very concerned about the high cost."*

Sales Rep: *"I think that's how I'd look at it, too – is the added quality worth the price? Would you like me to develop a proposal for this line and also for our laminate line? That would give us the exact cost difference we're looking at. You indicated that you will be here just three to four more years. I think that the numbers might show that you could recover the cost difference when you sell, meaning that you can enjoy the quality benefits I talked about before for only a little added cost. But let me put the numbers together for you, okay?"*

Customer: *"That would be great."*

Clearly the sales rep is doing benefit selling while educating the customer and helping the customer decide which product solution is in the customer's best interest. It's getting the benefits out onto the table that allows us to help the customer make a good decision about value (benefits) versus price or cost.

Selling benefits reduces the 'cost' in the customer's mind.

In fact, anytime you mention a feature, it's just as likely that the customer will be thinking 'extra costs' as it is 'more benefits.' Let me show you a model that really helped me understand this. The model is called the sales scale.

In determining whether or not to buy any product or service the customer is faced with a decision on price versus value, where he or she must weigh two things:

1. What will I get?
2. What will I have to pay?

We can visualize this like a scale.

If, in the customer's mind, price outweighs value, then there's no way a sale is going to be made. On the other hand, if in the customer's mind value clearly outweighs price, then the sale is going to happen. And if the customer believes that price and value are just equal…? Let's come back to that one.

The key to the sales scale is that the customer makes the evaluation of price versus value in her mind. Value is **not** in the product. Value is in what the customer **thinks or perceives** the product will do for her.

We could think of literally thousands of examples to validate this. Antiques have great value for some and are worthless in the eyes of others. To some car owners Toyotas offer greater value for the price than Fords; to others, the exact opposite is true. To some, caviar is worth its high price; to others it has no value at any price. Value is not in the product, but in how the customer **views** the product.

Truly understanding this can be one of the most important breakthroughs in your selling career! You can't change the products you are selling, but you certainly can change the way the customer perceives the product.

Think for a second about television advertising. What is the focus? Is it on educating you on the details of the product? Or is the focus on influencing how you feel about the product? The answer is obvious. In fact, most TV advertising is completely devoid of detail about the product.

The copywriter is trying to connect with you on an emotional level. At their best, they are brilliant. Do you remember the Budweiser ad where the Dalmatian acts as a personal trainer to get the young Clydesdale ready to join the big wagon pulling team? I love that ad, but what has it got to do with the taste or quality of beer? The point is, obviously, to influence the way you think about the Budweiser brand.

I think it's really hard, especially for a fairly technical salesperson, to realize that the customer doesn't really want or need to know much about the product itself. What they need to know is how comfortable it will make them, how much they will have to worry about its reliability, how it will affect their pocketbook, and how their friends will view their purchase.

Let's look at the sales scale again, but this time just at the left side of the scale.

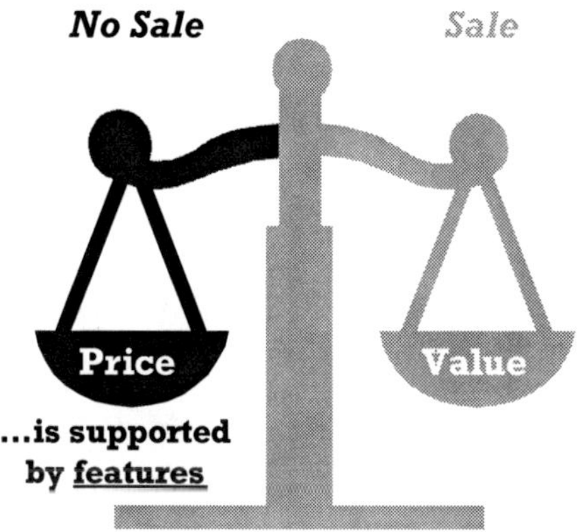

The language of the left side of the scale is the language of product **features**. Features and functions tell us what the product does, what it is made of, and how it works. In other words, the product's features really tell us why a product has the price that it does. It costs 'X' dollars because of the materials, engineering, quality, manufacturing, distribution and selling costs that have gone into it. Price is simply the sum of all these parts.

When we say something like, "*This is our most efficient model,*" we are also communicating an unspoken thought. That is, "*The price of this model is a direct reflection of the engineering, materials, and processes that had to go into this model to make it efficient.*"

When we are describing all the features of the product to the customer, what are we really doing? We're showing the customer why the product costs what it does. If we do a brilliant job of covering all the product features, where have we brought the sales scale? Back to the balance point.

We've proved that the price of the product is fair. But with the scale balanced, will the customer buy? They might. We just don't know. The problem is that features justify price but they don't necessarily add value in the customer's perception.

So what does add value? Benefits. The language on the right side of the scale.

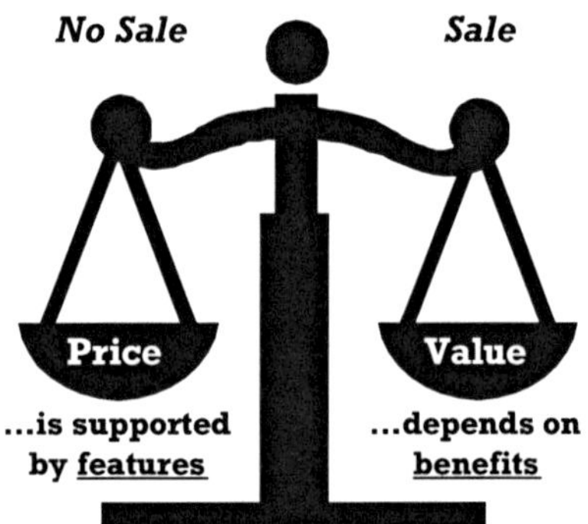

You can't change the price or the features, but you can change the customer's perception or understanding of the value of the product, since that is really a measure of what the customer **thinks** your product is going to do for him or her.

Helping the customer make a buying decision by adding value to the scale is what selling is all about. And, it is clear that the way to do this is to sell the benefits.

Feature selling gives the customer things to pay for.
Benefit selling gives the customer reasons to buy.

PRICE IS ONLY PART OF THE TOTAL COSTS TO THE CUSTOMER

The concept of presenting benefits and value is even more important than I've indicated so far. Look at the scale one more time.

There is really more to cost than price. The customer is really weighing the values of the product against the total cost of ownership. For the customer, price is only part of the total cost.

What other cost does the customer incur?

How about uncertainty and worry about the product doing what it's supposed to. ("*How do I know my utility bill will actually go down?*") How about 'opportunity costs,' the idea that whenever we do one thing we give up the opportunity to do something else? ("*If I give you this money, I can't spend it on a long weekend in Las Vegas.*") How about fear of the unknown? ("*How do I know that this product won't fail and ruin my day trying to get it fixed?*")

Let me try to capture this situation for you in a few simple sentences to be sure you appreciate how serious this problem is.

1. Buyers evaluate 'price' versus 'value' every time they make a purchase.

2. 'Price' is actually 'total cost.' It includes the price paid, but it also includes all the potential risks, like overpaying, being cheated, or getting a bad product.
3. Only benefits can overcome price and the other potential costs. The customer must believe that the benefits available outweigh all the possible reasons not to buy.

There's only one way to make a sale – the total perceived value to the customer has to outweigh the total cost to the customer.

Benefits don't always speak for themselves! It's the **sales rep's** job to stack value onto the customer's sales scale!

Assumption Number Two

Remember I said that there are two assumptions that salespeople make when they don't actually talk about the benefits of what they are selling. The first assumption is that if you tell the customers about the features, the customers will understand the benefits. This may or may not be true.

The second assumption is that if we tell the customers about the features, the customers will think about the benefits they will get. This is just plain WRONG. If we mention a feature, the customer is just as likely to be thinking **about** cost / price.

So what do we need to do? We need to actually say the benefits. In other words we need to get over our reluctance to 'sound like we're selling.' We are selling. All my experience says that customers respect salespeople who do their job as long as they believe that the salesperson is honest, trustworthy and working to help the customer make the best decision.

The second thing we need to do is to **add more value** whenever we can. Let me ask you a question. For any particular feature or function of a product, how many benefits are there likely to be? Just one? Is it always 'one feature equals one benefit?'

And your answer is probably… "*no.*"

In fact, do you remember I told you that I like to ask folks in my seminars to tell the group about the best thing they ever bought – the thing they were happiest about getting?

One attendee told us about his new $270 high-tech golf driver. This strikes me as a lot to pay for a club. When I first think about this, my own sales scale kind of goes 'clunk' over to the 'no sale' side. $270 just seems like too much money for a golf club. But then he starts talking about some kind of proprietary technology that somehow reduces spin as the ball flies off the tee so the ball rolls farther, giving you a longer drive. He goes on, "It's just a great feeling to hit the ball that far. I know I can lower my score one or two strokes. And I just love the fact that nobody else has one of these – my buddies are really jealous. This is the same thing the top pros are using."

Increased pleasure, lower score, pride of ownership, exclusivity – this thing is starting to sound pretty good. Maybe $270 isn't so much after all. I could just feel my sales scale tilting over to the 'sale' side while he was talking.

Whether the folks in my classes are talking about a boat or snowmobile, a golf club or a front loading washer – it's never just about one thing. It usually entails all the direct benefits of the product (like a lower golf score) and also the more subtle benefits of peace of mind, or pride of ownership. What they are describing is how multiple benefits put added weight on the sales scale – until the benefits clearly outweigh the costs.

Think about the sales scale as you read the two brief scenarios that follow. They feature two different sales guys, Rob and Bob, who both work for the same company. Their boss has instructed them to make their customers aware of a special offer they have. If the customer buys a furnace or air-conditioner from them they can obtain a $300 price reduction on an on-demand water heater installed at the same time.

Here's Rob:

Rob: "*Thanks very much for your order, Mr. and Mrs. Jones. I know you're going to be extremely happy with your new furnace and air-conditioner. You've made a good choice. Before I leave, I wanted to mention that my company also does have a special offer for our customers on our on-demand water heaters. Are you familiar with these?*"

Customer: "*No not really.*"

Rob: "*Well, it actually heats the water as you use it, so you literally can't run out of hot water. We normally price these at $1,495 installed, but we offer a $300 price reduction when we are already installing equipment. Is this something you would like to look at?*"

And here's Bob:

Bob: "*Thanks very much for your order, Mr. and Mrs. Smith. I know you're going to be extremely happy with your new furnace and air-conditioner. You've made a good choice. Before I leave I also wanted to mention that my company does have a special offer for our customers on our on-demand water heaters. Are you familiar with these?*"

Customer: "*No, not really.*"

Bob: "*Do you happen to recall when your current water heater was installed?*"

Customer: "*I think it was shortly after we moved in here, so that would make it 10 or 11 years.*"

Bob: "*Do you ever run out of hot water?*"

Customer: "*Only when everyone wants to shower at one time, and it seems like I'm always the last one!*"

Bob: *"The reason people run out of hot water is that tank type heaters like yours heat and then store a fixed amount of water. If you use it all up, the heater just takes some time to catch back up. The tankless units actually don't store hot water – they heat it as it's used, so you literally cannot run out."*

Customer: *"Hmmm."*

Bob: *"There are several reasons you might want to consider this. First, your existing water heater is nearing the end of its useful life. It will probably fail in the next few years – and you know they always seem to go at the worst possible time. Replacing it now would avoid that worry. It's just great not to have to worry about not having enough hot water – no more cold showers. And third, these are more efficient units. Since you're not storing hot water, you don't have the standby losses that you have with a tank-type unit, so it reduces energy cost. The burner itself is also more efficient, so that further reduces your gas bills. Lastly, we offer a $300 price reduction if you install one with your heating and air-conditioning equipment. Should I write up a proposal for you?"*

Customer: *"How much are we talking about?"*

Bob: *"The normal price is $1,495 so it would be $1,195. If your current unit does fail, that'll cost you $700 or $800 and energy savings is typically about $50 a year, so you're not really paying much more for continuous hot water and peace of mind. Should I go ahead and add that?"*

In the first scenario, Rob was told by his boss to mention the hot water heater special – and he's done that. *"This is the product; here is the price."* And the odds of closing this sale are remote at best.

In the second scenario, Bob probes for customer needs – how old is the existing water heater and do the customers ever run out of hot water – and he presents a solution. And he supports his presentation of that solution with benefits, such as freedom from worry, increased comfort, reduced energy costs, and reduced installation costs. The odds of closing this sale are pretty darn good.

Why? Because the salesperson is stacking value onto the customer's sales scale. The main reason not to buy – I don't want to spend the money right now – is offset with a whole bunch of benefits – comfort, freedom from worry, and energy savings.

This is the essence of benefit selling.

First, we don't **assume** that the customer will be able to translate our feature / function statements into benefits. We do it for the customer. We say the benefits.

Second, we don't **assume** that the customer will be thinking about all the benefits. We **say** all the benefits. We stack value onto the customer's sales scale until the value obviously outweighs cost.

That's our job, to stack on value at every opportunity.

WHEN DO YOU USE BENEFIT SELLING?

When do we actually do benefit selling? The simple answer is – whenever we can!

By now you certainly know that I'm not a big fan of 'pitch' selling. It's not the job of a professional salesperson to march into the home and announce, "*I know what you need and I'm here to tell you all about it, so just sit back and listen up.*"

On the contrary, the salesperson's job is to ask questions, listen carefully, and educate the customer. Through this process of dialog with the salesperson, the customer will be able to clarify his or her needs, and the salesperson will be able to make the best possible proposal.

So how does benefit selling fit into this professional process?

The T.R.U.S.T.® selling process and 'benefit selling' are 100% compatible. Talking about the benefits of a product or service is **not** pitch selling. On the contrary, the more you think of the customer as an individual who has unique needs that require the best possible solutions, the better you will be at benefit selling. We can't effectively communicate the most meaningful benefits unless we understand the individual customer's needs.

As long as you keep your focus on the customer, you can and should be using the skills of benefit selling at every stage in the sales process. This means during the greeting, during the questioning or 'discovery' phase, during the presentation of your proposal, and during the discussion of any customer concerns following the first closing attempt.

As long as you are focused on the customer, and not on you and your product, these benefit selling skills will make you more effective. Let's look at the use of benefit selling at various stages of the sales call.

USING BENEFITS TO STRUCTURE YOUR PRESENTATION

You are probably the only salesperson who your homeowner customer is going to see who comes into their home and spends significant time asking a series of questions about their needs and wants.

You could just introduce this concept to the customer by using a straightforward explanation like this:

"In order for me to give you the best possible proposal, I need to spend a little time surveying the job and I also would like to ask you a few questions. Is that okay?"

Or, you could improve on this professional straightforward approach by using the skills of benefit selling. What will the **customer** get out of the process? Here's how you might say essentially the same thing – but with a better customer focus.

"We have a lot of different product solutions that might possibly fit your requirements, and I want to be sure I propose the ones that best fit your specific situation. In order to do this I need to make a detailed survey of the physical job requirements. But more importantly, I need to understand exactly what you and Mrs. Smith see as your most important requirements and desires. Do you have time right now for me to ask you a few questions to help me understand exactly what you would like to see in the new system?"

In the first scenario, the salesperson assumes that the customer will see the benefits of a more customized proposal. The second scenario makes it more explicit by telling the customers that the proposal will be customized to their specific situation.

With a little more thought about your product offering and its potential benefits, you could make your opening even stronger, like this:

"We have a lot of different product solutions that might possibly fit your requirements. Some of the key differences are going to be in the way they affect your personal comfort and your future energy bills. I want to be sure that I propose solutions that give you the best possible combination of comfort, energy savings, and out-of-pocket costs. Here's what I've found is the best way to do that. I need to do a detailed physical survey of the job requirements. But more importantly, I need to spend some time with you and Mrs. Smith to be sure I understand exactly what you folks would like to see in a system. Do you have some time you can spend with me right now?"

So here's an idea for using benefit selling right from the start of your sales interaction.

First, think about what you **really** sell – not the product – but what you really sell: comfort, energy savings, peace of mind, increased home value, less work, and pride of ownership. Then, ask yourself if there is a way to bring these benefits right up to the front of your sales interaction.

This will keep you focused on benefits. And, it will build the customer base interested in working with you.

USING BENEFITS TO STRUCTURE YOUR DISCOVERY QUESTIONS

The questions that you ask, including the questions on your survey form, should be created with benefits in mind. These are all good benefit oriented questions:

- "*Do you plan to stay in this home for more than a few years?*"
- "*Is there anything about your current system that you'd like to see improved?*"
- "*Are there areas of the home that are less comfortable than others?*"
- "*Does anyone in the home suffer from respiratory conditions?*"
- "*How do you feel about the current cost of heating and cooling your home?*"

I think you can see how the answers to any of these questions could lead to this benefit oriented discussion:

Sales Rep: "*Do you plan to live in this home for more than a few years?*"

Customer: "*Right now our plan is to stay here at least another six years until our youngest finishes high school. Does it make a difference?*"

Sales Rep: "*Actually it can be an important issue. Sometimes you can pay just a few dollars more up-front – but get additional energy*

	savings that will actually return your investment in two to three years – and then give you money back."
Customer:	"*What kind of difference are we talking about?*"
Sales Rep:	"*After we complete the job survey, I'll be able to work up a couple of different proposals for you that will show you exactly what the numbers are and what kind of return you'd see, okay?*"

EDUCATING THE CUSTOMER BY USING BENEFITS

At just about any point in your sales call – but especially during the discovery phase – you're going to have a chance to educate the customer. You're entering a **dialogue**. You'll ask a question, and more often than not the customer will come back with his or her own question.

For example, if you ask, "*How long do you plan to remain in the home?*" it's very likely the customer will want to know how that affects his choices. If you ask, "*Are there any problems with your current system that you'd like to have corrected?*" it's very likely the customer will ask whether you can address a certain type of problem.

These are opportunities to educate the customer on possible solutions, as well as get a better feeling for how customers view these possible solutions. Is this something that they might be willing to invest in?

In almost every case the customer will not know as much as you do about the product or service you are selling. If they did, why would they need you or your expertise? It's your job to give them enough information to make an informed decision without overwhelming or confusing them.

As I said earlier, I've trained thousands of heating and air-conditioning salespeople. These ladies and gentlemen tend to be quite knowledgeable, but also fairly technical. I have never met a homeowner who wanted to know exactly how a scroll compressor differs from a piston compressor or exactly how a variable speed furnace differs from a single stage unit.

Doing effective benefit selling is the key to successfully merging a technical, knowledgeable salesperson and a non-technical customer. If we start off explaining exactly how the two furnace models are different, we're done for. We need to start by explaining the benefits.

"*You said that your current system is noisier than you'd like – especially when it first comes on. The reason for this is that your current furnace is either off, or it's on. You hear it turning on and off all the time. We do have a unit that works differently. It starts at a very low speed and then speeds up and slows down to provide heat – but you don't hear it because it's not turning on and off. So it's a lot quieter. It saves money on energy too because the heat output isn't swinging up and down as much.*"

If the customer is satisfied with your broad answer – that you can reduce their noise problem – then you can leave it there. And, if the customer wants to know more detail he or she will ask.

USING BENEFITS TO SUPPORT YOUR PROPOSAL

In Chapter 4, we talked about the 10-step sales call, which included reviewing your proposal. I suggested you include additional information, such as company background, information on licenses and insurance documents, pay back calculations, etc. Each of these items should be covered briefly with a focus on the key benefits of each item.

"*This is a copy of our mission statement. You can rest assured that we'll do whatever it takes to ensure your total satisfaction.*"

"*This is our contractor's license. This means you won't have to worry about whether we have complied with all local requirements.*"

"*This is one of the roofing lines that I'm going to propose to you. This line will give you the long life you're looking for, and the appearance will match the style of your home. I think he will be very pleased with the way your home will look.*"

Keep it brief and emphasize the benefits. The customer will ask if he or she wants more detail.

USING BENEFITS TO RESPOND TO CUSTOMER CONCERNS

Benefits are the key to your response. And here's a critical point. If you have not gotten the key benefits onto the table by this point, you have a problem. If you have gotten benefits on the table, then you'll be able to say with confidence things like the following:

"*I can put together a system at any investment level, but I know that you did want to do something about your excess humidity and also improve air quality, and I wouldn't want to see you not get those benefits.*"

You need to have covered the key benefits before you ask for the order so that you can remind the customer what it is that they **are getting** with your proposal, and what they would **not be getting** with a less expensive solution or with another supplier.

Get those benefits onto the table! Don't be afraid to sound like you are selling – you are!

CHAPTER 7

Handling The Bumps In The Road: What To Do When Customers Object

One of the most amazing experiences that I have when I am the customer is when a salesperson actually tries to **argue** with me. I'm sure most of us have had this kind of experience. I'll make an innocent observation like, "*Gee, that seems kind of pricey,*" and the salesperson comes back with, "*Tom, you have to understand what goes into something like this.*" I have to understand? Well, excuse me!

Sure, we don't get paid unless we make the sale so when someone says something that seems to block our progress toward the sale, we want to push it aside, or run over it, because it's in the way. That's exactly the wrong thing to do. What causes salespeople to act either defensively or aggressively when they encounter any kind of resistance?

An awful lot of salespeople still view selling as something that the salesperson does **to** the customer. They see it as a competition; they want to win and will do what it takes. This is win-lose thinking… and it's wrong.

Selling is helping **the customer** find the best solution to a problem. Selling is not something we do **to** the customer. It is something we do **with and for** the customer. This is the heart of T.R.U.S.T.® selling – developing a relationship with the customer based on honesty and an understanding of the customer's specific situation.

Salespeople who use T.R.U.S.T.® selling clearly see themselves trying to serve the customer so bumps in the road are not threats. They are simply bumps, and it is our task to help the customer get around or over the bump. We are certainly not going to accomplish that by telling the customer that they, "Have to understand."

So how do we deal with these bumps in the road? In most selling courses this subject would be called 'objection handling,' and I'll use that phrase as well. I want to clarify, though, that each time a customer shows any sign of resistance it is not necessarily an objection. The customer may just be expressing doubt about something, asking for clarification or even just thinking aloud.

As an in-home salesperson you're going to get two fundamentally different kinds of objections. First there are the minor 'speed bumps' that can arise at literally any point during a sales call. Here are some examples:

- "*I don't care for that style.*"
- "*That looks too complicated.*"
- "*I've never heard of that brand.*"
- "*I'm not interested in anything that requires maintenance.*"
- "*A friend of ours had a less than positive experience with your company.*"

Second, there are the 'not yes' responses to your attempt to close. When you ask your closing question some customers will say yes and you should expect that. Many, of course, will say something else. My experience is that homeowners may use a lot of different words and phrases to respond to your closing question when they are not yet ready to proceed, but 99% of these responses boil down to just four objections:

1. "*I want to think about it.*"
2. "*It's too much money.*"
3. "*I can't afford it.*"
4. "*I need to get other bids.*"

Regardless of whether we hit one of the minor speed bumps, or one of the four 'no, not yet' pot holes, the fundamental process for addressing them is the same. So let me give you some basic objection handling tools.

OBJECTION HANDLING TOOL NUMBER 1 – PREPARATION

As we have already discussed, you cannot understand an individual completely unless you can establish a positive relationship that allows you to probe their wants and needs via questions and careful listening. Sometimes the feedback you get will be neutral, such as "*Our monthly utility costs are $180.*" Sometimes the feedback will be positive, such as "*I like that idea.*" Sometimes the feedback will be negative, such as, "*I don't think I should go with just one proposal.*"

An objection is not a rejection. It's a gift. It's the way the customer gives you feedback. It all helps you understand the customer's thinking. It all helps you see what you need to do to help the customer move toward the best solution for his or her problem.

There is a 100% certainty that you're going to get objections on sales calls, and under most circumstances these objections are not personal. The homeowner is not upset with you, doesn't dislike you, and is not trying to keep you from doing your job. Customers have, in fact, good valid reasons to raise objections:

- Customers do not want to part with money unless they are virtually certain that value will be received. (Do you remember the sales scale?)

- Customers, like all of us, tend to resist **any** change. Even if the customer invited you into their home, and even if they know they must act to solve their problem or fulfill their desire, they may find it hard to take action.
- Emotion and prejudice do exist. Things simply look different to different people.
- Real problems do obviously exist, like size, style and budget constraints.

Not only do you know that you are going to get objections, but you also can **anticipate** what specific objections you are most likely to get. I just listed the four most common 'not yet' objections: I need to think it over, it's too much money, I can't afford it, and I need to get another bid. We'll go into those in detail, but you can easily anticipate other objections that you will get and take similar steps to ensure that you are completely prepared to address them.

For example, if you sell product lines that are not household names, you should be prepared to explain why you use those lines and have the evidence to back you up. If you are going to make any product superiority claims, have the evidence you need to back them up in your briefcase. If your work is disrupting to the home itself, arm yourself with photos that show how careful your installation crews are and also how they leave things after the installation.

It's really just common sense. The more photos, case studies, and technical support you have in your briefcase, the more prepared you are to respond to any objection.

OBJECTION HANDLING TOOL NUMBER 2 – THE SKILL OF DISARMING

There is simply no place for arguments in handling objections. **Never** let an objection become an argument.

We just talked about the fact that customers have legitimate reasons for raising objections. They are a form of feedback. Why would you ever get into an argument if your attitude is that "*I want to be sure I understand why you might have some concerns before you are ready to move forward, so can we talk about those concerns?*"

The purpose of the **disarming** step in handling objections is to prevent an argument from occurring. We prevent objections from becoming disagreements by:

- Showing the customer that we are not trying to avoid the objection.
- Showing the customer that we are trying to understand his or her point of view.

There is a specific disarming technique that is nearly always helpful. This is to use a statement that agrees that the customer is right in his position, or agrees with the importance of the customer's concern. It usually doesn't agree with the objection itself.

I cannot tell you how often I use the technique of disarming, but it's often enough that by now it's just kind of built into my DNA. I really don't even have to have to think about it.

Let me give you an example. I do charge a fairly large daily fee for the work I do with customers when I am holding training meetings. So I'm quite used to the 'sticker shock' reaction. I know in my heart that my fee is justifiable and reasonable, but I also know that if I leap immediately to that justification we could end up arguing about it. So when customers say, "*Boy, Tom, that's a lot of money,*" the first thing I say is, "*You're absolutely right, Frank, it is a lot of money and I know it is a large investment for your company.*"

My disarming statement agrees with the customer's position that this is a lot of money, and it agrees that this is an important concern. It does not agree that it is too much money. That is an important differentiation.

Similarly in training sessions I know that there will be the inevitable argumentative question. My first words in response will be, "*That's a very good question, and an important one.*"

Here are some examples of good disarming statements:

- "*I can see your point.*"
- "*I can certainly appreciate your concern.*"
- "*I'm glad you raised that point.*"
- "*Cost (style, size, etc.) is certainly very important.*"
- "*It is a large investment.*"
- "*I can appreciate that. I'm the same way about major decisions.*"

Each of these statements shows concern for the customer's point of view without conceding that the objection itself is correct.

Some sort of clarifying question or statement should follow the disarming phrase. What happens if you take any of the phrases above and follow them with the word 'but?'

- "*I can certainly appreciate your concern, but...*"
- "*I'm glad you raised that point, but…*"

It certainly puts the phrase in a different light, doesn't it? Instead of disarming the objection, it says to the customer "*I don't really see your point of view; this is just a technique I've learned and now I'm going to tell you why you're wrong.*" Avoid the word 'but.' Resist the natural tendency to defend your point. It's not about being right. It's about helping the customer understand that their concern need not prevent them from achieving the solution they would like to have.

So it's all about your mindset. You can't act like you truly want to understand the customer's concerns and help him or her deal with those concerns, unless you really do. Once you have the right attitude, then you understand why disarming is such a helpful tool. It starts you down a positive, non argumentative road toward dealing with the customer's concerns.

OBJECTION HANDLING TOOL NUMBER 3 – THE SKILL OF CLARIFYING OBJECTIONS

Time and again, when a customer raises an objection, a sales representative will jump to answer what he or she believes the objection to be without giving the customer a chance to explain what he / she really means by the objection. Here's why is it so important to get the customer to clarify his or her actual objection.

First, it's almost impossible for a salesperson to judge the seriousness of an objection unless the salesperson draws the customer out and gets the objection into its proper perspective.

Second, if the objection has an emotional aspect to it, most customers cannot sustain any length of emotional outpouring when they're discussing the details that lie behind the objection they have raised.

Third, the customer gains respect for, and confidence in, the salesperson as he or she demonstrates a willingness to hear them out instead of blocking their effort to say what's on their mind.

Fourth, the customer may not really have thought through the objection, and in clarifying their position, they may actually answer the objection themselves or at least put it in perspective.

And fifth, and probably most important, the salesperson must be sure that both he and the customer understand the customer's actual objection.

Let me show you an example of clarifying an important objection before attempting to respond to the objection. I'm going to use the 'too expensive' objection that we might well get after we ask our closing question.

Let's start by looking at a scenario where our guy Joe fails to either disarm or to clarify the customer's objection:

Joe: *"The cost of the complete project is $6,270 or, if you were to finance that, it would be $185 per month. Which is better for you folks?"*

Customer: *"Wow, that's way more than we expected to pay."*

Joe: *"Well, you do need to look at everything that we're going to do for that amount. Let me back up and point out what we're including. First..."*

And Joe is off and running… and what's happened? Well, first, Joe has missed the opportunity to close and has re-launched himself into a re-presentation of his proposal.

Second, he has deprived the customer of a chance to speak up about his feelings. Not only does this mean that Joe may not understand the customer's objection, but it also leaves the customer feeling pressured.

And third, Joe may just convince the customer that it **is** too much money.

Joe really mishandled this. Let's give him another try, except this time let's have Joe at least disarm the customer's objection.

Joe: *"The cost of the total project is $6,270, or if you were to finance that it would be $185 per month. Which is better for you folks?"*

Customer: *"Wow, that's way more than we expected to pay."*

Joe: *"I know that it is a large investment, and one that requires some thought. Maybe it would be helpful for me to go over some of the key benefits for you. First, this is our most energy efficient system and you did say that energy costs..."*

At least Joe disarms the customer's objection and acknowledges that this is a large investment. Without clarification he again loses his opportunity to close and simply re-launches himself into his presentation.

So let's give Joe one more shot, but this time insist that he both disarm **and** clarify the customer's objection before proceeding.

Joe: *"The cost of the complete project is $6,720 or, if you were to finance, that it would be $185 per month. Which is better for you folks?"*

Customer: *"Wow, that's way more than we expected to pay."*

Joe: *"I know this is a very large investment. When you say it's more than you expected to pay, are you talking about the total amount, or the monthly payment?"*

Customer: *"No, we could swing the payment if we had to. It's just a lot of money."*

Joe: *"Like I said, it is a large investment, but you know it is just that... an investment."*

Customer: *"Is there any way we can get the price down a bit?"*

Joe: *"You know, we can design a system at just about any price point. Setting aside the price for a second, how do you feel about the system as I've proposed it? Does it include the things that you'd like to have?"*

Customer: *"I do like what you've proposed, especially the higher efficiency equipment."*

Joe: *"If I flip back to the energy savings calculations that I showed you, you can see that you actually save over half the system costs in energy savings during just the first five years of operation, and the system literally pays for itself in energy savings over its life."*

Customer: *"Ummmm, yes, that's true."*

Joe: *"Would you like to go with this?"*

Disarming and clarifying the objection keeps Joe in the closing phase of the call. By pinning down the customer's concern that even though he can afford it there's a real sticker shock involved, Joe has the chance of showing the offsets to the cost. Now he can try to close again. If he fails, then he can back up and talk about removing elements of the system. At least he's given the customer a way to think about the investment, and he may be able to close the project as presented.

This particular example is not an uncommon situation. I'll bet you can think of times when your own first reactions to something like that new boat, car, golf club or dining set was that it was really expensive. You ended up buying it anyway. This sticker shock issue is especially common in the in-home selling environment simply because people don't know what a lot of the stuff we sell might actually cost. This is one of the key reasons I suggested that you quote a choice of solutions. It helps the customer put price into perspective. But price is often going to be an issue, and so we need to know how to treat the objection.

You need to disarm. You need to clarify. You need to understand whether the objection is a bump in the road or a roadblock. If it is just a bump in the road, let's work around it. And if it's a roadblock, we can go back and justify or modify the proposal as needed.

These three tools – preparing, disarming, and clarifying – apply to the handling of any objection.

HANDLING THE FOUR MOST COMMON OBJECTIONS FOR HOME SELLERS

When I first started to develop a training program for in-home sales people, one of the most surprising things was realizing how few responses there are to an in-home salesperson's closing question. Ninety-nine percent of the time you're going to get one of just five responses. The customer is going to respond with some form of 'yes' or one of the only four objections. Since there are only four, we certainly should be well prepared to deal with them. I listed these earlier:

1. "*I need to think it over.*"
2. "**The price is too high.**"

3. "*I can't afford it.*"
4. "*I need to get another bid.*"

I'm going to spend the rest of this chapter going over the best way to handle each of these 'no sale – yet' responses.

OBJECTION: WE NEED TO THINK IT OVER

It's extremely common for homeowners to try to delay answering your closing question. There are several reasons for this.

First, some people just don't like to make large decisions, so they try to delay. And, most in-home purchases are big decisions. Normally, you are asking the homeowner for a significant investment. Customers know that they need to decide in order to get a solution to their problem, but they don't want to be hasty. In addition the amount of your proposal will often be higher than expected or hoped for. It's only normal to try to delay.

Second, couples often need time to talk alone. They don't want to have a discussion in front of a salesperson. And neither one wants to say something that the other might not agree with.

Third, homeowners may have an unspoken objection, especially one of price or affordability that they're not ready to share with the salesperson.

When I am with a salesperson and they get this kind of delaying objection – "It's a big decision; we're going to need to sleep on that" – I'm always disappointed when the salesperson just gives in. I can't tell you how many times I've heard the response, "I can understand that. When would be a good time for me to call and see how you're doing?"

You do **not** want to drop the call immediately when you get a delay type of objection. The customers did not say that they need some **infinite** amount of time to think it over, so why not just assume that they only need a very **brief** time? It sure can't do any harm.

The best way to prepare for this objection is by having an excuse in mind that will allow the customers a few minutes alone to see if a decision is reachable. Here's an example:

Homeowner: "*It's a big decision. We're going to need to sleep on that.*"

Sales Rep: "*I can appreciate that; my wife and I are the same way. We like to take some time to think over big decisions like this. Can you help me understand what you might be thinking about?*"

Homeowner: "*No, we just need time to think about it.*"

Sales Rep: "L*et me suggest this. I'd like to call my scheduler and see what the openings are for the next few days. It should take me just a few minutes. I'll call from my vehicle and check back in about 10 minutes to see if you'd like to go ahead – or if you need to sleep on it. Okay? At least I'll be able to let you know what our installation schedule looks like.*"

OR

Sales Rep: "*Let me suggest this. I need to go take some final measurements that we'll need at some point, so let me take 10 minutes to do that and you folks can chat about this. Okay?*"

First the salesperson disarms the objection and then asks a clarifying question. Then the salesperson gives the customer an option of discussing the decision in private.

I like the technique of checking schedules or checking product availability or taking final measurements, as it actually gives the homeowner some additional information whether they decide now or not.

Return in 10 minutes and try to close again. You could save a sale.

It's also possible that when you ask the customer your clarifying question you might clarify that there is, in fact, a different objection, like this:

Sales Rep: "*I can appreciate that; my wife and I are the same way. We like to take some time to think over big decisions like this. Can you help me understand what you might be thinking about?*"

Homeowner: "*Well, frankly, the total is a lot higher than we anticipated. It's more than $2,000 over our first bid.*"

Well, at least we uncovered the real objection and now we can handle it directly.

OBJECTION: YOUR PRICE IS TOO HIGH

From the salesperson's perspective, this is potentially the most emotional of the common objections. It can look like a challenge to your integrity. You know that you have priced the proposal correctly and may be inclined to leap to your own defense. Don't. Here are the facts.

First, your proposal is probably higher than the homeowners expected or hoped for. The homeowners have not had an opportunity to adjust to the reality of price versus value.

Second, if the homeowner is comparing your proposal to another contractor's proposal, yours may well be significantly higher. The homeowners don't have all the information they need to compare the two proposals correctly.

Third, homeowners don't know how contractors price. They may believe that contractors are like car dealers, and that they will get a discount if they simply negotiate.

It's very important to disarm this objection. Money is a big deal to folks. Your disarming statement agrees that it's a big deal and one that you're not afraid to discuss honestly. You need to use a phrase like…

- "*It is a big investment.*"
- "*You are absolutely right. It's a significant investment.*"
- "*Cost is always an important consideration.*"

After your disarming statement, you need to be absolutely sure whether this is a concern about the **total cost**, or is a concern about the customers being able to afford the **monthly** cost. The best way to do that is to ask the question, "*When you say the cost is too high, are you thinking about the total cost, or is it more the amount of the monthly payment?*"

Usually this question will get a response that clarifies whether this is a true price objection or a concern about affordability. The customer might say, "*It just seems like more than I really want to pay,*" or they might say, "*I just can't afford that in my monthly budget.*" We'll cover the latter in the next section.

So, how do we handle the true price objection? I recommend that you have four solid principles in mind.

First, you are the expert on price. You know why the job costs what it does. The customer does not.

Second, the price is the price. You set the price fairly to make a fair profit and you're not going to cut it, unless you change the content of the proposal.

Third, you can design a system or a job at just about any price point, but that means leaving out features and benefits.

And fourth, just about everything that in-home sellers sell is intended to last for an extended time meaning that it has both a first cost **and** a total life cost.

If you live by these principles you can take pride in your proposal, and you can explain it without being argumentative or defensive.

So how do you apply all that? Let's have our sales guy, Joe, handle a price objection and then expand on the techniques that he is using.

Homeowner: "*That's way more than we expected to pay.*"

Joe: *"I can certainly appreciate that. It's a significant investment. Is it the total investment or the monthly investment you're thinking about?"*

Homeowner: *"Well, we could afford it, but it's over $1,000 more than our other bid."*

Joe: *"Would it be helpful if I went over some of the reasons that it costs what it does?"*

Homeowner: *"It might."*

Joe: *"Let's go back and look at the things you said were most important. You said that energy efficiency was very important, and also noise level, even temperature control, eliminating winter dryness, and so is doing something to fix the lower-level temperature control. The system I designed takes care of all of these, but obviously there is a cost associated with each one."*

Homeowner: *"I can appreciate that, but can't I get the job done for somewhat less money?"*

Joe: *"Let me assure you, we can give you a quality system at just about any investment amount but with fewer benefits. Before we talk about any lesser system though, let's look at some numbers. $6,270 is a big number, but not compared to your overall system operating cost. You'll actually spend about $30,000 over the life of the equipment to run it. If we look back at this energy summary, you'll see that you will actually save about $4,000 in the next 10 years just in energy use, and that's assuming that energy costs don't increase. If we dropped back to lower efficiencies, we could get you a lower first cost, but you'll pay it back to the utility. I have Energy Star calculations for similar systems in this market, and the difference in cost typically equates to about 25% return on your money."*

Homeowner: *"I see your point."*

Joe: *"Pay now, or pay more later. Should we just go with this system?"*

Homeowner: *"How about some of these other items? Can we take those off without impacting what I'm getting too much?"*

Joe: *"Sure, we could do that, but you'd lose the benefits. I think in each case were talking $20-$30 a year over the system life. One of the things you said was that the family gets a lot of colds and the house seems drafty in winter. If the new system helps them, what's that worth? In total you are going to pay about $100 a year extra to get a system that's best for your family's needs. It's up to you. Do you think you want to address all of your problems or look at cutting back to a lesser system?"*

Going back to one of my very first sales training classes, we learned a technique called ad – subtract – divide – multiply. That's what Joe is doing here.

He is **adding up the benefits** that the homeowner will get with the proposal.

Then he's **subtracting the benefits** the homeowner will not get with a lesser system.

He's **dividing the price differences** into smaller increments.

And, he's **multiplying by the intangible values** like quality, peace of mind, etc.

This is the technique that Joe uses here.

Joe takes away the values you don't get in a less expensive system. I really encourage you to memorize the phrase, "*I can design a high quality system for you at just about any investment amount, but with fewer benefits.*" Does the homeowner really want to give up energy savings to reduce up-front costs? She needs to be asked to make that decision. It's her choice.

Joe uses the life cycle costing concept to help the homeowner see the up-front cost in relation to total operating cost. The customer is not just buying a $6,000 system; they are gaining $4,000 in energy savings. The price difference isn't $1,000; it's about $100 a year. No one would have a coffee at Starbucks every day if they thought of that as a $1,000 investment, but at $3.00 a day it's okay.

Joe even multiplies the value of his proposal by the intangible of better health, "*If the system helps, what's that worth?*"

So that's how you handle a price objection. Add the values you get for a higher price. Subtract the values you lose with a less expensive solution. Divide the price into the smallest units you can. And don't be afraid to talk about the intangibles. What are peace of mind, health, comfort and pride of ownership really worth? Give your customers this information and let them **choose** what's best for them.

OBJECTION 3 – WE CAN'T AFFORD IT

I never like to see anyone make the mistake of buying something that they truly cannot afford. The customer will have regrets, and the customer will resent the salesperson who encouraged them to make a poor decision.

On the other hand, I hate to see someone not get the best solution they can get for their money.

By this point, I'm assuming that you have internalized the T.R.U.S.T.® selling process. Our job is to develop enough of a **relationship** with the customer to be able to **understand** the customer's needs – including financial needs. A person using T.R.U.S.T.® is going to make a proposal that fits the customer's needs. We're not going to propose a Mercedes to a customer who honestly needs a Saturn.

But even a Saturn costs a lot of money. And in-home sellers must have adequate understanding of financial, as well as product, solutions.

If you sell solutions that are literally worth thousands of dollars, then you must have a sound understanding of two areas – financing, and return on investment.

Hardly anybody pays cash for major investments. Any company selling expensive products like heating and air-conditioning, remodeling, roofing, or windows has to be able to offer the homeowner some kind of financing option. Of course, that's the basis of your alternate choice of finance close, "*The system as you've laid it out is $6,777, or if you were to finance that, it would be $180 per month. Do you want to finance that, or would you pay it directly?*"

This isn't really something you can do yourself as an in-home salesperson. It's really up to your company to provide you with some kind of finance solution. That might come through a supplier, through a utility program, or through a relationship with a local bank. Your job is to make sure your boss understands why you need such a tool, and make sure you get it. You wouldn't go to a car dealer who couldn't help you with financing; you can't expect your customers to buy from you if you can't do the same.

Returns or pay back can offset up-front costs for the homeowner. If you spend money on your home, there are at least two potential areas of return on investment that could help you offset part of the up-front cost.

The first one is energy savings. This is an obvious one. Every dollar you can save on energy is a dollar in your pocket. How would your finances be affected if you could spend an extra $1,000 to reduce your annual energy outlay by $200? Well, in five years (or sooner if the cost of energy were to go up) you'd get back your $1,000. You'd have a five-year pay back or a 20% return on your investment. After 10 years, you'd have avoided at least $2,000 in energy costs for an investment of $1,000. Is this a good deal? Of course it is – especially if you can borrow the original investment (by financing the job) at, say, 7 or 8% interest. Who would not borrow money at 8% interest to earn a tax free return of 20% on that money?

If your customer is concerned about affordability, and there is energy savings involved, that's the first place to go. It's real, and it's significant.

I would start by reminding the customer of the total energy savings. If your proposal saves $200 per year in energy, and the homeowner plans to stay in the home for at least 10 years, that's more than $2,000 in savings.

I would also try to compare the return on the added investment to other alternatives that are available to the customer. If the customer is going to pay cash, you need to point out that current returns on savings accounts are only a few percent – compared to X% on the energy savings investment. And, if the customer is going to finance the job, then any energy savings higher than the borrowing cost represents positive cash flow back to the customer.

You also need to be an expert in any other areas related to energy costs. This might include the involvement of any outside players. Are there any utility rebates available? Is there any preferential financing available for higher efficiency equipment? Are there any tax savings or credits available? It can all help reduce the out-of-pocket cost to the homeowner.

Besides energy costs, I think in-home sellers need to understand the area of 'life costing.'

Higher quality can save money.

The total cost of any home improvement includes the up-front costs, the cost to operate the improvement over its life (mainly energy costs), the cost to maintain the improvement over its life, and the cost to replace the improvement at the end of its useful life. I've already talked about energy costs, which could be many times the initial system cost. You should have a good handle on the other aspects to the degree that they impact what you are selling.

An improvement that lasts twice as long as a lower quality alternative has half the annual cost on a life cycle basis. Longer life can add to the value of the home at sale time if the homeowner does move. An extended warranty can have a dramatic impact on potential service costs. All of these differences can be brought to bear on the 'affordability' issue.

There are some specific techniques that are useful in handling the 'can't afford it' objection. When you get this objection, here's the procedure I recommend you follow.

First, as with any objection, be sure you use a disarming phrase such as, "I can appreciate that – it is a big investment," or simply "I know it's a lot of money."

Second, clarify the situation. Remember, with a price objection you need to know whether the customer could afford the investment, but thinks the price is out of line, or whether the customer doesn't see how they could afford to pay that amount of money. So we always ask.

Here's another example with our friend Joe. Let's see how he handles this objection.

Homeowner: "*That's just more than we can swing, Joe.*"

Joe: "*I can appreciate your concern; it is a lot of money. Can you tell me, is your concern related to the total price, or are you looking at the size of the monthly payments?*"

Homeowner: "*Well it's both, but we just can't afford that kind of monthly outlay. Our budget wouldn't handle that.*"

Joe: "*It might be helpful to look at the energy savings because they are significant. We calculated that it would be a savings of at least $30 a month in energy costs, and that reduces your monthly outlay to about $150 a month. Is that more affordable?*"

Homeowner: "*It helps, but it's still too high.*"

Joe: "*Had you planned to pay part of the cost in cash or to finance it all?*"

Homeowner: "*Originally we were thinking it might cost around $4,000 to replace the old system, and we were going to pay half and put half on our home equity line of credit.*"

Joe: "*Obviously that would make a big difference. If you still put $2,000 down you'd only be financing a little over $4,000. I assume your home equity rate is pretty low?*"

Homeowner "*It's about 8%.*"

Joe: "*That's even a bit lower than the Energy Star rate that I was using. The interest is deductible I take it? I have a table here. Let's see, $4,277 at eight percent for 60 months is only $87, and $30 of that will come from utility savings. Only $57 a month for five years for the best system for you. Is that something you'd like to go with?*"

Joe clarifies that this is an affordability issue. Based on that he uses energy savings as an offset to price, and he helps the customer analyze financing options as well.

What if this is still not affordable? Well then we need to bring the cost down by working openly and honestly with the customer to subtract the benefits that will have the least importance to the customer.

OBJECTION 4 — WE NEED TO GET ANOTHER BID

I'd say the first thing you need to do when you get this objection is not to take it personally!

Most homeowners intend to and believe they should get multiple bids. The exception, of course, is a customer who contacted only you as a result of a personal referral. (Wouldn't it be nice if they were all like that? Why do you think it's so important to close the sale and get a referral or a future call from your old customers?)

But, alas, they're not all referrals. And so we need to deal with this expected 'bump in the road.'

As I said, it's not personal. Customers have been trained to do this. They have not been made aware of the differences between a high quality, customized proposal and 'another bid.' Even if you've done a great job of clarifying that difference, they may still believe they need more bids. Or, they may be saying this because they've already lined up one or more additional companies to make a proposal.

My attitude is this. I've done the best possible job I can of working with you to clarify your requirements. This is a high-quality proposal. It fits your needs. It's fairly priced. I think you should go with it, so why shouldn't I press just a bit if I feel this is a good solution for you.

Let's go back to Joe one last time and see how he handles this objection.

Homeowner: "*Joe, you've done a nice job putting this together and we appreciate that. It's a lot of money – and we feel like we should talk to at least one other contractor before we make a decision.*"

Joe: "*I can understand that completely. It's a big decision. Many of my clients do get more than one proposal – and many don't. Can I ask what you would primarily be looking for in speaking with another contractor?*"

Homeowner: "*I guess mainly price. This seems like a lot of money to spend without a comparison.*"

Joe: "*I see. Actually, we not only help you design a good system – but we also shop the price for you.*"

Homeowner: "*How's that?*"

Joe: "*A lot of our business comes to us via referral – as you did. In order to earn that kind of trust we need to make sure each client gets the best possible job – and also gets a fair price. We benchmark ourselves continuously against the other good contractors not only on price but on installation quality and overall customer satisfaction. In fact, after we complete your system we'll be asking for your feedback, and will also be asking for referrals if appropriate. We couldn't operate that way unless we actually provided the best value for the price on every job. I do honestly think this is the best system for you, and that we can save you a lot of time and effort by proceeding now. I'd love to put you on our schedule."*

Homeowner: "*I sure believe you, Joe, but I just wouldn't feel comfortable going ahead without some kind of comparison.*"

Joe: "*I'm fine with that. I do want you to feel like you're getting a top value, which I know you are. As long as you are comparing apples to apples we will be very competitive. I would be more than happy to go over the two proposals side by side to help you make that comparison if you would like.*"

Homeowner: "*I do appreciate that, and I will give you a call.*"

So that's it.

Prepare for objections before the call. **Disarm** and clarify objections before you respond. Do not be defensive, but remember that **your job is to help the customer** understand whether the objection is a roadblock or just a bump in the road that the two of you can get around.

CHAPTER 8

The Natural Conclusion: Bringing The Call To A Close

Most in-home sales people only get paid when they make a sale. Their ability to take a lead and convert that prospect into a real customer is literally the difference between making a living and not. Given that, one would expect that in-home salespeople would be pretty firm closers. They are not.

Any salesperson who has ever participated in sales training has been taught that the most important thing in selling is to ask for the order. In spite of all the attention, and encouragement, we know that many salespeople do not try to close. In fact, closing is perceived by salespeople as being one of the most difficult parts of their jobs. In an international survey of sales representatives, more than 35% identified closing as their number one sales concern. In a study conducted through records kept by buyers at a major industrial firm, 47% of salespeople who called on that company did not attempt to close.

Let me give you some real life data specifically about in-home salespeople. At the time of writing this book I have had the opportunity to train more than 7,000 in-home sales folks. In every seminar I have asked the same question. "How many of you ask for the sale on every sales call?" Less than 1 in 10 asks for the sale every time! Nine out of ten salespeople who make their living and support their families by selling don't ask specifically for an order on each sales call. Incredible.

If you ask salespeople why, the most common answer is that they don't like to close so they avoid it. They enjoy the customer interaction and rapport that is built up during the sales interaction. They like finding out about the customer and her needs, and they enjoy talking about their product and their sales proposals. They don't like having to ask the customer to buy. They don't want to mess up a good relationship or pressure the customer to buy. They **fear being rejected** with a 'no.'

I've given more thought to this issue than any other. If I could just get folks to ask for the order I could raise their effectiveness and help them make more money.

HERE IS WHY YOU MUST TRY TO CLOSE

Start by recognizing that 'no' is not a personal rejection. If you see a no as a personal rejection then it's natural to fear closing. Let's face it, when you attempt to close on **every** call, over half the time the customer's initial response is going to be something other than 'yes.' If you consider every one of these non-agreement responses to be a personal rejection, you're going to be pretty depressed. Under those circumstances it would be natural to stop trying to close unless the customer seems like he wants to grab the pen out of your hand.

I won't even call these 'not yes' responses negative. They are simply feedback providing more information you need in order to proceed. What you've learned is that the customer isn't ready to sign your proposal yet. So what are the reasons? That's what you need to find out. It doesn't mean you're not going to get this sale eventually. It simply means that right now the customer has some concerns that need to be addressed.

Sales professionals who attempt to close on every sale by asking a specific closing question understand that they are asking for **any** response. Sure, they hope that the response will be yes, but there's a good chance it will be 'no, not yet.' Either way, they understand the need to get a response.

If you don't attempt to close by asking a specific closing question, four things happen, and they are all bad.

First, the customer doesn't get the benefits of the system you are proposing. It's true that the customer hasn't decided to buy from you, but after thinking it over and possibly comparing your proposal to other bids the customer may still come back to you. But, it's also possible that the customer will simply go with another supplier – possibly one who just asks at the right time.

Second, you are going to waste some valuable selling time. Regardless of whether you eventually get this business or not, the fact is that you're not getting it right now, and you will need to invest some additional time later, possibly even requiring another visit to the customer's home.

Third, you're going to lose some self esteem. It doesn't feel good driving away from a sales call thinking, "*I know I did a good job for these people. I bet I could have wrapped them up.*"

Fourth, you are going to reduce your income. This is just a fact. If you don't attempt to close, you will reduce your close rate, which will directly reduce your earnings.

Let's say that you make your proposal and the customer likes what you have proposed. However the cost is more than the customers expected, and they are not sure they can afford it. You don't know that because you didn't ask. If you did ask, the customer could say, "*Well, we like your proposal, but we're not sure we can swing it.*" This would allow you to help the customer look at areas like energy savings or different payment methods. Maybe the fact is that with your help they would see that they actually could swing the expense, but you didn't ask. Instead, you ducked the question. You said something like, "*Why don't you folks look this over and I'll give you a call Thursday evening and see if you've had a chance to make a decision. Okay?*" The next day another contractor comes in, offers a lesser solution at a lower price, and gets the business.

The reason you need to attempt to close is to find out what the customer is thinking so that you can try to help them deal with any questions or concerns.

It doesn't matter whether they believe your proposal is too costly, or simply believe that they can't afford it, or they just have a hard time with large decisions or they have other salespeople lined up. It doesn't matter which it is, because you can't do anything about it anyway. You didn't get that information because you didn't **ask**. It's a fact that if you don't find out what's on the customer's mind, you will lose some sales that you could have closed if you had just asked!

HERE'S HOW YOU CAN CHANGE YOUR CLOSING BEHAVIOR

Here's my thinking about exactly why people don't like to close and how you can change that for yourself.

Let's say that you decided to volunteer to help out with a political campaign, so you show up at the local office for your favorite candidate. They ask you to do some phoning and they give you a list of numbers to call. You, quite naturally, would ask, "*What do we know about these people I'm calling?*"

Let's say the answer was, "*These are some of our best supporters. They have contributed money to our guy. We just want you to remind them about the upcoming rally, and ask them to please go to the candidate's websites and consider contributing again.*"

No big deal, right? These people will not object to hearing from you. You might even enjoy chatting about your common interest in the candidate. When you ask them to please visit the website, most will say, "*Sure, no problem.*" You can easily do this.

Let's assume, instead, that the answer to your question regarding what we know about these people is, "*We really don't know much. We think most of them will be for our opponent. We want you to try to get them to at least visit our candidate's website and check it out.*"

Are you kidding me? You can't do that. These people do not want to talk to you. About half the time you're going to face rejection. People will say nasty things to you. People will hang up on you.

The upshot is that if we know people generally agree with us, and possibly even like us, then it's going to be easy to ask them to take some action. We aren't nearly as willing to ask someone to take action if we think that person might reject us and maybe even get nasty about it.

Now let me apply this to our in-home selling situation.

If you just spent a half hour with the customer dialoguing about that customer's needs and desires; if you seem to be hitting it off and you sense that the customer would really like to work with you; if you have gotten continuous positive feedback from the customer on your various suggestions and ideas; if all that is going for you, wouldn't you feel pretty comfortable asking the customer to go ahead and sign your proposal?

On the other hand, if you have greeted the customer at the door, but have spent the last 30 minutes surveying the job alone; if you have not engaged in any question-listen-question activity with the customer; if you don't know if you are the only bidder or just one of several; if you have no idea whether the customer would like to work with you or not, wouldn't you feel somewhat reluctant to use a direct closing question? Because you **fear rejection**? Lacking an established relationship is almost like a cold call isn't it?

I think this is exactly what happens in selling. If you have a **relationship** and a complete **understanding** of the customer's needs, and if you have an idea **how your customer is feeling** about your proposal, it's easier to close. If you have no relationship, do not have a good understanding of the customer as an individual, and do not know exactly what the customer is feeling, it's going to be tough to close.

The closing question comes near the end of the call. Successful closing actually has more to do with what happens at the **beginning** of the call than it does with what happens at the **end**! Do you remember back in Chapter 3 where I talked about the three phases of the selling process and about the idea of the T.R.U.S.T.® inverted triangle? We said that every sale has the same three phases. In phase 1, 'Approach with Discovery,' we work to understand what the customer needs. In phase 2, 'Prepare Choices,' we prepare alternatives that will address the customer's needs. In phase 3, we 'Present, Propose and Close' to get an agreement from the customer to take action. Far too many sales calls look like this triangle:

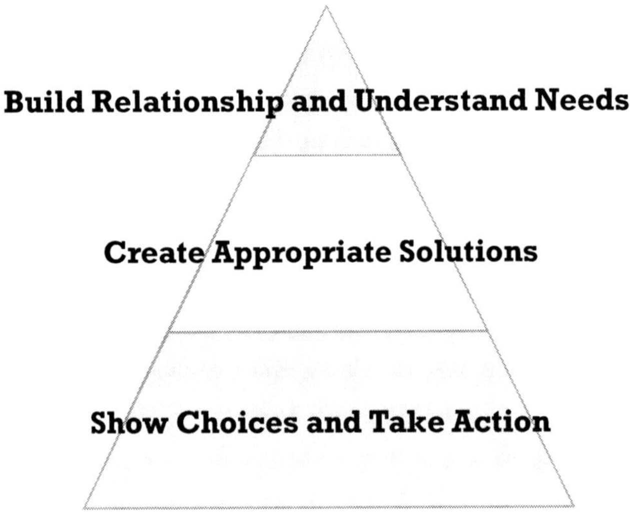

Phase 1, when we determine what the customer needs, is typically very short. It is not uncommon for it to be as short as this example:

Salesperson: "*Hi, I'm Frank Jones from ABC Heating. I understand you folks called to have us come and look at a new system for you.*"

Customer: "*That's right.*"

Salesperson: "*Great. Well I know you're busy so I'll try not to take too much of your time. If it's all right with you, I'll be walking around the house taking measurements and looking at the current system.*"

Customer: "*Fine.*"

With that, the salesperson is off to survey the home and put together a proposal.

'Approach with Discovery' was essentially non-existent.

Admittedly, after the physical survey, the salesperson will know quite a bit about the home, the current system, maybe even something about the customer's lifestyle. He won't know anything about the customer's desires, knowledge level, biases, budget concerns, etc.

So in reality the sales rep is **flying blind** with regard to the specific needs of this customer.

Let's keep going now with our example to see how this impacts the salesperson's ability to close. The salesperson, after his brief introduction to the customer, and his physical survey of the job, creates a proposal with appropriate choices that he is guessing will satisfy the customer's needs.

At this point, the salesperson knows that phase 3 – Present, Propose and Close – is going to be very long and very difficult. The sales rep reviews the proposal that the company usually makes for this **general type of customer.** Following this proposal the salesperson is supposed to ask for the order. At this point, the salesperson does not know whether this offering really fits this customer at this time because he never determined this customer's **specific** desires, needs, wants, and constraints. The customer may feel pressured. They may raise numerous objections. All in all it's not an easy situation. Too often the salesperson will simply avoid this anticipated unpleasantness altogether.

How comfortable would any salesperson be asking for the order when they don't know if it's the right thing for the customer, or whether or not the customer is open to the offering?

Salesperson: "*So that's the proposal. Do you have any questions? If not, why don't you think about it and I'll call you in a few days to see if you had a chance to decide whether you'd like to go with it or not. Is that okay?*"

This failure to close effectively is not an issue of knowing **how** to close. It is an issue of not **understanding** the entire sales process. Sales reps fail to close because they have no idea whether their customers are ready to buy! Their 'Approach with Discovery' is too short; their 'Choices Proposal' is too generic; and their 'Close' is going to be difficult… and most of the time they simply choose to avoid it.

The secret to closing is to invert the triangle! Your sales process has to look like this:

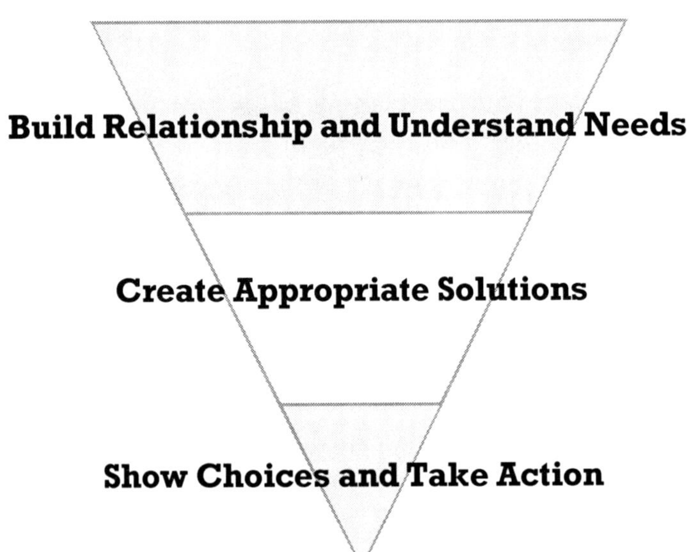

THE T.R.U.S.T.® SELLING PROCESS AND CLOSING

If you follow the process taught in this book, the T.R.U.S.T.® selling process, you **will** close. It's the natural, and comfortable, conclusion to your call.

You'll have a survey form, or at least a set of questions, that you will ask the customer. This will force you to spend **time** with the customer. It is this time together that establishes the **relationship** with the customer and is also the foundation of your **understanding** of the customer's needs. You'll put together a choices proposal that will show the customer exactly how your recommendations fit the customer's needs. The last page of your proposal will be detailed financial information with a total investment and a monthly finance investment estimate.

I suppose it is still theoretically possible for you to get cold feet even at this point and use what I referred to as the 'cop-out' closing question, "*So that's my proposal for your new system; is there a time when you'd like me to follow-up to see if you've made a decision?*" But now you won't do that, because you know that would be a disservice to the customer and a tragic waste of your extensive effort.

So you'll close, by asking the customer for a choice decision. After all, it's not a '**TRUS**' selling model. It's a '**T.R.U.S.T.®**' selling model, and the final '**T**' stands for **T**aking action.

HOW YOUR COMPANY PRESENTATON BOOK HELPS YOU CLOSE

When I walked you through the selling process steps in Chapter 4, I talked at length about the company presentation book. Ideally your 3-ring, easel backed book (or computer based presentation, if you prefer) will have these sections:

- Information about your company

- Information / photos about how you do your work
- Information about your licenses, insurance, etc.
- Collateral material that supports your company, people and products
- Applicable technical material, like energy savings projections
- Information about the products you intend to propose

The company presentation book is a value-adding closing tool. I assume this is obvious to you, but let me repeat the message that is delivered to your customer by the material you'll cover in your presentation.

- "*I want to tell you about my company because we're going to be working together, and I want you to feel confident in our ability to do a good job for you.*"
- "*I want to tell you about the kind of work we do because companies aren't all the same, and you should know how our work compares to others.*"
- "*I want to tell you about our licenses, insurance, etc. because you shouldn't have to worry about something going wrong.*"
- "*I want to show you some of the important, non-product benefits we offer because you're going to get more than just a new product with your installation.*"
- "*Finally, I want to show you the product choices I propose that best fit what you've told me you want.*"

Think about it. After all that how can you possibly **not** ask the customer if he or she would like to go ahead with the proposal?

One of my great disappointments as a trainer is that I know from experience how many salespeople will attend my training (or read this book), agree with everything I'm saying, and then not take the time to put together their proposal tool… their **closing** tool.

Please, for your sake, and for your customers' sake, do it!

IT'S EASIER TO CLOSE IF YOU HAVE A PERSONAL 'COMMITMENT TO ACTION'

What's your reaction to this interchange between a salesperson and a homeowner?

Homeowner: "*What's the main reason for the difference in price between these two window lines? They look the same to me.*"

Salesperson: "*They have different quality glass. They are both good, but this line has a special coating that blocks sunlight better during the summer to help keep the house cooler and, of course, that reduces air-conditioning costs.*"

Homeowner: "*Interesting.*"

Salesperson: "*Yes. It's quite the technology.*"

My reaction is that this is an opportunity missed. This kind of educational interchange can lead directly to a sale. Here's how:

Homeowner: "*What's the main reason for the difference in price between these two window lines? They look the same to me.*"

Salesperson: "*They have different quality glass. They are both good – but this line has a special coating that blocks sunlight better during the summer to help keep the house cooler. And of course that reduces air-conditioning costs.*"

Homeowner: "*Interesting.*"

Salesperson: "*Um hmm… it's quite an advance in technology. Is that something you would like me to include on a proposal?*"

Homeowner: "*Well, maybe. How much energy savings are we talking about?*"

Salesperson: "*The manufacturer has documented savings 10 to 15%. You mentioned your annual cooling cost is about $1,000, so that would save you about $100-$150 a year. And the cost would be in the range of a thousand dollars, so you'd recoup your investment in around six years assuming energy costs keep rising. That's about a 16% tax-free return on investment. How does that sound to you?*"

Homeowner: "*I think that would be worth it.*"

This salesperson just 'trial closed' a $1,000 addition to his proposal.

Some sales training books call these 'trial closes or test questions.' I think it's easier just to think of it as having a 'commitment to action.' You're trying to help the customer get somewhere. The customer has needs. You have a wide variety of possible solutions. You want to help the customer find the **best** solutions. So every time you give the customers some new and important information, you have the opportunity to determine whether the customer thinks that's important. You need to ask if they would like to have that. The answer will nearly always be 'yes.' And, my friends, the road to making the sale is paved by hearing the word 'yes!'

Here are three features and their benefits.

- "*This line of roofing has a 40-year guarantee. Not only does that give you a lot of peace of mind, but it adds to your home's resale value when you do sell your home in the next few years.*"
- "*This unit modulates the heat, rather than turning it on and off. This does two things: increases comfort, and reduces noise.*"
- "*These cabinets have extra strong frames and hinges. They are designed to last a lifetime even in a home where they have the hardest use.*"

On a stand-alone basis these are just pieces of information. A seller who is committed to helping the homeowner reach the best possible decision needs to understand how the homeowner views each of these. Does this fit your situation? Would you want to pay for it? To determine these answers, we need to ask a 'trial closing' question even though we're in the middle of the call:

- "*How do you feel that might work in your case?*"
- "*Is this something you'd be interested in?*"
- "*Would you like me to work up a return on investment number on that?*"
- "*I know you're moving in about three years, but it still might make sense to consider this. What's your thinking about that?*"

This is a commitment to action. It's obvious how it helps us at the close. We've **already closed** on key elements of the proposal. Think of these as baby steps… with each step you are moving that much closer to making the sale.

THE CLOSING QUESTION ITSELF

There are a lot of books with a lot of closing techniques. I don't like the 'hard close' techniques one sees when they go to buy something like a new car. You know, the bit where they take your driver's license and won't let you leave until you've spent some time with 'the boss.' In fact, my sense is that even the car dealers are dropping these kind of approaches. These techniques clearly have no place in in-home selling.

I don't want you to be a 'hard' closer, but I do want you to be **committed to closing**. If you don't close, your customer will not get the product or service that is best for them. If you do not close, your own time may be wasted, costing you income and the personal satisfaction that comes with doing a good job.

So how do you close, without being too pushy or aggressive? I advocate just two specific closing techniques. One is the 'direct' close. The other is the 'alternate choice' close.

THE 'DIRECT' CLOSE

Simply asking the customer to agree to move ahead is open and honest: "*If this looks good to you, may I go ahead and set up the installation? This matches up exactly with all those things you said were very important. With your okay right here we can get you going.*"

The direct close makes the most sense when the customer has given very strong buying signals. You could certainly use it as your standard close. The disadvantage, if you want to call it that, is that a direct close will get an equally direct response. That could be a direct confirmation, "Okay, let's go with it," or it could be a direct negative, "*No, I'm not ready to do that yet.*"

This is not a problem for the salesperson who is mentally prepared and confident in her selling skills. She simply disarms the response, "*I can appreciate that; it's a big decision,*" and, then she clarifies, "*Could you tell me what it is about the proposal you're thinking about?*" With that she's back into the selling process.

THE 'ALTERNATIVE CHOICE' CLOSE

The direct close is straightforward and professional. Many buyers see it as a logical extension of the process. After all, isn't it the salesperson's job to close? Still, there are probably quite a few people who might find it a bit abrupt. For that reason a lot of sales folks prefer a 'softer' alternative choice close. Sometimes referred to as the 'positive choice' close, this close simply asks the customer for a decision about some aspect of the order rather than asking for the order itself.

In closing, we are really making an assumption that the customer has already made a mental decision that value outweighs cost. In other words, we're assuming that the customer's sales scale has already tipped over to 'buy.' The alternate choice close is very compatible with this idea. It simply asks the customer something about how she would like to go ahead with the action, assuming it has already been decided that she is going to proceed.

The closing question doesn't ask whether the customer will give us an order, or take some other action, but rather asks some detail about the order. These questions could be where, when, who, or how type questions – although not necessarily using those words.

- "*The total is $4,687, or if you were to finance, it would be $87 a month. Which of those would work better for you?*"
- "*We could begin installation next week, or if you prefer we could wait until after the holidays. Which would you prefer?*"
- "*We work with either Jones or Smith as installation subcontractors… do you have a preference?*"

For in-home sellers I do think that the alternate choice finance close has a lot of advantages. This close, the first of the three examples just above, simply states that the total investment is X, or the monthly investment is Y. "*Which is better for you?*"

Here is why I like this close for in-home selling. The alternate choice finance close immediately shifts the customer's focus from total cost ("*Wow! That's a big number!*") to incremental investment ("*Well, at least it's affordable if we take one month at a time.*") It is very likely that your proposal will be higher than the homeowner originally expected. This is largely because when the homeowner called you, she was originally just thinking 'heating and air-conditioning' or 'new windows,' and you've demonstrated the benefits of energy savings, better air quality, increased comfort, reduced noise, longer life, return on investment, etc. The customer wants these benefits. But getting them is going to make the purchase somewhat more expensive than she originally thought.

The alternate choice finance close supports a key part of your sales story in that this purchase is an **investment** and not just a cost. The finance close, by emphasizing monthly investment, reinforces the investment / pay back story. If the customer does raise one of the four anticipated objections ("*That's more than we can afford*") it leads naturally to your follow-up ("*Is it the total investment or the monthly investment that you're thinking about?*") If it's the monthly outlay, we can immediately reinforce the things that impact the monthly bill or can transition to other ways to address the affordability – including down payments, different loan terms and so on.

The alternate choice finance close reinforces that you can solve all the customer's concerns, which include financing. Can you imagine going to a car dealer, a store, or even a restaurant, that didn't offer some kind of credit arrangement? As a seller directly to consumers, you need to offer some way to help the customer with finance concerns. This close reinforces that you do address the financing concern. You have financing; why not let the customers know that you offer it?

The alternate choice finance close can simplify the sales job. This close does fit every sale, whether it's $2,000 or $12,000. You can use it on every close. This can help you increase your closing attempts to 100%! It simplifies your presentation as you always know how it's going to end. You can use the same language on every call. It increases your effectiveness; with practice it becomes very natural so you do it better and better.

The alternate choice finance close is professional and low pressure. Unlike a direct close, which can get a direct negative answer, this close is a 'soft' close. If the customer is not ready to say 'yes,' they don't have to say 'no' either. They can simply accept your close as another piece of information, i.e. the cost of this proposal, as it stands is $4,687, which equates to a monthly payment of $182.

THE BEST-BETTER-GOOD CHOICE® PROPOSAL AND CLOSING

I believe strongly that in almost every case your proposal form should be structured to show the customer three alternative solutions, or choices, all of which can meet the customer's needs. I discussed this at length in Chapter 4, and if you don't recall all the reasons why I think this is so important, I hope you'll flip back and review.

The purpose of showing multiple choices is simply to help put the price in perspective with other higher-featured or lower-featured solutions. The alternative solutions also communicate instantly to the customer what happens if he doesn't want to pay that much. He can see that he can have a less expensive solution, but with reduced features and benefits. If you're selling products that can cost thousands of dollars you need to have some way of helping the customers to evaluate price.

In addition, we need to remember that many of our customers may also have price impressions from other companies. If our competitor is at $10,000 and we are at $13,000, then we look out of line. If we offer systems at $14,000, $12,000 and also a basic system at $10,000, we look like we are competitive, except that we are offering the customer choices with more value.

When you close with multiple solutions on your proposal form, you should not initially use an alternate choice close that asks the customer to select the solution they prefer. You want to convey clearly that, based on your interaction with the customer and with your knowledge of their needs, you have prepared choices for them to consider but would like to recommend the best choice first.

"*So, based on what you've told me is important to you, I've prepared three choices for you to consider. They are all very good. Even the basic choice is significantly better than what you currently have, and customers who choose that one are very happy. However, our best choice would provide the most benefits to you. May I have permission to explain that one to you first and then we can answer questions about the others?*"

Trust me, your customer will say 'yes!' Then proceed explaining how the best choice delivers solutions and value and ask for the sale:

"*So, seeing how our best solution will do the best job for you, do you think the total investment or the monthly investment would be better for you, or would you like to talk about the other two system choices?*"

Remember our discussion on styles? Some people have decided already that they will buy and you don't want to run the risk of turning them away by droning on about things that are no longer relevant. Ask and they will buy! For the rest you've now given them a choice – buy or learn more – and either answer they give you is still leading you toward the sale.

Selling with T.R.U.S.T.® – and giving customers a CHOICE®. It works.

AFTER YOU ASK FOR THE ORDER

It's often said that once you ask your closing question, if you speak first, you lose. I'm not sure that's always true. You can work your way back to another closing attempt, but why would you want to do that? You put the question on the table. Now wait. The customer has been asked to commit. It might take her a moment, or even several minutes, to make up her mind. Be respectful, give her time to think… and wait until she's ready to speak.

Once the customer agrees to buy, or agrees to whatever action you suggested, don't keep selling. You might end up 'buying it back' by opening the door to further objections that did not come up before. So after you get the order:

- Reassure the customer that she did the right thing.
  - "*I'm confident that over the next few months you'll really be glad you decided to do this.*"
  - "*Congratulations, Mr. and Mrs. Smith, I think you've made a very wise investment.*"
- Handle the paperwork details as briefly as possible.
- Explain what will happen next, such as who will be calling to schedule the installation or which installers will be coming out to their home.
- Remind them you are available at any time they might have questions.
- Confirm that you will be re-contacting them after the installation is done (or that you may be there to start the installation with your installers).
- Thank the customer.

At this point you could depart. It is a good point to mention other products or services that your company offers which did not come up earlier in the call. You have completed your first sale. I think it's fine to try to lay the groundwork to a second sale that could begin right now or that could lead to a future call. You can refer back to Chapter 4 where I discuss this final step.

This is also a good time to make it clear to the customer that you always are seeking, and are appreciative of, referrals. I go into more detail about this in the next chapter.

CHAPTER 9

Creating Your Future: How Rich Do You Want To Be?

I like to end each of my seminars with two things. First I provide a checklist of 'next steps' or a roadmap for the future. Second, I ask each attendee to write down some specific actions they are going to take as soon as they get back on the job.

Albert Einstein said that the definition of insanity is doing the same thing over and over again while expecting a different result. Do you want different sales results? If the answer is 'yes,' then you have to do different things. So I ask people to commit to doing those things that are most likely to help them start getting different, and better, results.

These last two chapters are my attempt to do that same thing in this book – to help you think about the material you've read and to bring everything down to those specific actions that you can take to be more successful. This chapter looks at the bigger issue of where you might want to take your selling career. Chapter 10, 'Staying in Momentum,' asks you to identify some of the key short term actions you could take to move forward. Let's start with the big question of how far you personally would like to go in your professional life.

This book teaches a process – the T.R.U.S.T.® selling process. The system itself is sound. It works. Here's why.

The highest earning in-home sellers earn more than their peers for one of three reasons:

- They get more chances than their peers.
- They close a higher percentage of the chances they do get than their peers.
- They produce more dollars per sale than their peers.

T.R.U.S.T.® selling is built on those time tested and proven principles that correlate directly to selling success.

First, T.R.U.S.T.® sellers do get more chances. Anytime we can establish a personal relationship with someone we increase the chances that that person will refer a friend or relative to us. People don't refer others to companies just because they do a good job. They refer others to you because you do a good job, because they trust you, because they like working with you, and because you asked for a referral. That's why T.R.U.S.T.® sellers get more chances and more referrals.

Second, T.R.U.S.T.® sellers do close a higher percentage of sales than their peers. T.R.U.S.T.® sellers 'invert the triangle.' The more time we spend up-front with the customer, the more we dialogue, educate, and develop a personal relationship, the more likely we are to close the sale. Plus, we ask! It's built into the process.

Third, T.R.U.S.T.® sellers do produce more revenue – and profit – per sale. It's simply ridiculous to think that everyone needs the exact same thing. They don't. If we make each customer aware of **all** the possibilities available, some will choose the 'good,' some will choose the 'better,' and some will choose the 'best.' Any customer who picks either the 'better' or the 'best' is going to get more benefits for themselves and at the same time it will be more profitable for your company.

Thousands of sales professionals have already improved their sales results using T.R.U.S.T.® selling. How well it works depends on how committed each individual is to making it work. Some people get modest results. Some get great results. Some get rich. That's not a direct function of the process alone. It's a function of how much effort each individual puts into making the process work.

So the first question is, "*How successful do you want to be?*" Do you want to improve your results by 10%? 100%? Or do you truly aspire to the loftiest heights that are achievable in your particular sales field? I have met many in-home salespeople who do very well. Some earn literally twice as much as their peers. I also know a few in-home salespeople who earn much more than that. How is that possible? There are only so many hours in a week, so many weeks in a year.

This has always fascinated me. What do these super salespeople do that is **different** from everybody else? How can others do that? In this chapter, I'm going to tell you.

It's not rocket science. Some of the wealthiest salespeople do not have college degrees. They are no smarter than you or I. As the old football saying goes, "*They put on their pants one leg at a time, just like you and me.*"

They are just richer.

I'm going to refer to these rich salespeople as 'super sellers.' I don't know if you want to be one of these people or just be more successful than you are now. Either way, you can learn from what they do. So read this next segment with an open mind. Assess your own abilities and personal desires. At the end, I'll give you some guidance on developing your own personal 'next steps.'

So here's how super sellers do it.

The most successful in-home salespeople do **three things** that are distinctly different from their peers. They **work especially hard**. They **set goals**. They **market themselves** so they actually become their own 'brand.'

THE SUPER SELLERS WORK HARD

Saying that anyone could work harder is the exact same thing as saying that anybody could be more fit. It's undoubtedly true that anyone can be more fit than they currently are, and most people could achieve a reasonably high level of fitness if they wanted. It simply comes down to choices. You have to choose the salad rather than the burger. You need to hit the gym instead of the bar with friends. You need to ride the bike instead of watching the game. Those are hard choices. Each of us ends up with the set of choices, and therefore the fitness level, that we are 'okay' with.

The same thing is true of hard work. We know what it looks like. And, we also understand the trade-offs that are involved. We'd have to give up things that we like, such as more leisure time, to do more work. What happens is that we make these choices over time. They come to define us.

A number of years ago, a major manufacturer did a very interesting experiment. They knew that they had very high performing territories with highly paid reps and very low performing territories with lower paid reps. They wanted to understand exactly why. So they actually swapped salespeople. They took salespeople from high performing territories and put them into lower performing territories and put salespeople from low performing territories into high performing ones.

I bet you can guess what happened.

The salespeople from the high performing territories immediately improved their new territories to the degree that they quickly got back to their prior high compensation levels.

The sales reps from the low performing territories let their new territories slide backward. They were heading right back to their prior lower compensation levels.

It wasn't the territories... it was the salespeople. Some wanted that higher compensation, and they did what was needed to get it. Some were satisfied with lower compensation and did only enough to get by at that level.

If you really like what you are doing, and really would like to make a lot of money, I can tell you that the choices you make will pay off. But it will strictly be up to you to make them. No one can do that for you.

I will say this. In selling it's particularly important to work **both hard and smart**. It's often not as important to put in long hours as it is to stay very focused on the opportunities to sell! If the best time to reach your prospects is in the evening and on weekends, then you need to sell every evening and every weekend. You can take your time off during the day, but you have to be available when the customers are available.

Here are three specific ways that the highest earning salespeople work smart.

Work Smart Tip Number 1:

Adjust Your Schedule to Your Customer.

The ideal in-home sales call reaches all the decision makers at one time. This usually means both husband and wife. In addition, the ideal sales call is closed in one call (or two calls if a lengthier proposal preparation phase is required). If you only reach one decision maker, then you are doomed to a delay. "*I'll have to run this past my spouse.*" So you need to adjust your schedule to your customers. It won't happen the other way.

Work Smart Tip Number 2:

Be Absolutely Prepared.

You can't close on one call unless you're absolutely prepared. The question that you can't answer… the piece of literature you don't have… the proposal form you forgot... any of these could cost you another call. How much valuable selling time does that cost?

An image that I like to use is that of an operating room. These folks are going to put someone to sleep and open them up. They can't afford to 'forget' something. They are prepared for literally any eventuality. They very seldom mess up.

A good in-home sales presentation looks like an operation. It's been thought through. Every tool is prepared and is where it belongs. There is an air of competence and professionalism. That is the kind of preparation that's required.

Work Smart Tip Number 3:

Make, Verify and Keep Appointments.

I've worked with a lot of contractors. One of the worst feelings was to show up after a long drive only to be told, "Oh, something came up and Mr. Jones isn't in right now." I never could decide if I was angrier with Mr. Jones or with myself. It was usually my fault. Did I have an appointment? Yep. Did I arrive right on time? Usually very close. Did I remember to call and verify everything was set? Well... maybe I missed that.

Here's how to set your in-home sales appointment. Begin with confirming an exact time. Then use this opportunity to set up your exact expectations and help the customers to clarify what they can expect as well.

"I've found that I can do the best job if I can meet with both you and Mr. Jones together so that I have a really good understanding of what you folks would like to have. The process usually takes about an hour. If I got there right at seven o'clock tonight would you both be available?"

Or, if you are concerned about offending a woman by suggesting she can't make a decision on her own:

"I'll be happy to come by tonight at 7:00. I'll ask you some questions, write down what is most important to you, make a brief survey of your home, with you preferably, and then be prepared to show you some choices to consider. If there is anyone else you might wish to join us, anyone who may also have questions, please feel free to invite them. Does all that sound okay?"

Second, follow-up. Things change. It's your fault if you miss that. Call several hours before the appointment. Verify that you are on schedule and make sure the customers are as well. If something has come up you can reschedule and avoid a wasted call.

And third, be exactly on time. It's polite and it's professional.

THE SUPER SELLERS SET GOALS.

You will accomplish what you set out to accomplish.

Setting goals produces results. Period.

I said that super sellers do three things. They work hard and smart. They set goals. They market themselves. If you just work hard, work smart, and set goals, I'll just about guarantee that you can earn twice as much as the person sitting next to you.

I had the advantage of working for a large company when I first started selling. We had 'management by objectives.' Every year I had to list the five or six top things that I was to accomplish that year. Then every quarter I would meet with my boss to assess my progress. You know, that works!

Those are the two necessary characteristics of a good goal. It has to be **achievable** with some good effort. And it has to have a **timeframe**.

Now that I work for myself, I still set goals and I still review them to see how I'm doing. For an individual like you or me, setting four or five key goals is probably sufficient. Consider having two or three performance goals and one or two developmental goals.

Performance goals keep us focused on the big stuff. For a small company there might be a goal for total annual revenue and another for income. There might also be a major non-financial performance goal such as attending two self improvement workshops each year. There might be a few major developmental goals, such as getting a book published or pursuing a new kind of work. If it isn't written down with a date attached, it probably won't get done.

Goals demand strategies.

When you write down a goal that you think is achievable with some good effort by a certain time, it forces you to ask the next question, which is, "***How** the heck do I do that?*" That is a 'strategic' question.

A strategy is a statement of how a goal is going to be accomplished. For each of your key written goals you should also be able to write down a simple strategy. If you have a goal to increase your total sales by 10%, and I ask you, "In general terms how would you get that kind of increase?" you would answer with your basic strategy. For example, strategies for creating a sales increase of 10% could include: make 10% more calls, increase my close rate by X percent, increase my average sales per close by 10%, or some combination of these strategies.

Similarly, if you have a developmental goal to sell three times more of a target line, how are you going to do that? Approach new customers? Quote it more consistently? What's the strategy?

Goals demand **strategies** which demand **plans**. Strategies are broad 'how' statements. Plans are specific statements of the what, where, and when that support the strategies.

Here's what I know from experience that is specific to your success as a salesperson.

1. You have to **write down** your top three to five goals each year.
2. You have to **write down** your main strategy (or strategies) for accomplishing your top goals.
3. You don't need to spend a lot of time writing detailed plans, but you do need to at least **put key target dates on your calendar.**

Here is an example of exactly how you would do that.

Let's say your top goal is to increase your personal sales by 10% this year. Write that down on a goal sheet.

You determine that your best strategy to do that would be to increase your average dollars per sale by 10%. Write that down on your strategy sheet.

You determine that you'll need some new tools to help you do that – especially a different proposal form, and the new survey form. To accomplish your goal, when would you need these tools in place? Put those dates down on your planning calendar! And meet them!

If you do that, you'll make the goal. If you don't do that, you'll wake up a year from now and find that you didn't develop a new proposal form, didn't develop a new survey form, didn't increase your average dollars per close by 10%, and didn't accomplish your number one goal.

In the appendix to this book I have included examples of a simple goal setting sheet and also a strategy sheet. You can use these or something similar. The key is to use something to write them down.

THE SUPER SELLERS MARKET THEMSELVES AS A 'BRAND'

Safeco, Starbucks, Mercedes-Benz, Cheerios, iPod... these are all brands. Sometimes they are company names, sometimes the names of products, sometimes just symbols like the star on the grill of your new Mercedes.

Someone has put a lot of time and effort into marketing the brand. That means they have worked hard to influence the way people think about those names or symbols.

Brands don't have to be national or even regional. They can be very local. As I said, I spent more than 30 years selling, and much of that was in the heating and air-conditioning industry. In larger cities there might be hundreds of dealers, and if you stop someone on the street and ask them to name one, they couldn't. Then there are the exceptions.

My first large employer worked with a contractor in Cincinnati, Ohio. That dealer was a household name in the entire Cincinnati market area. He was a **brand**. There are dealers in Seattle, Minneapolis, Syracuse, and Orlando who are known to thousands of people. These dealers have marketed themselves as brands. Their names have meaning to people.

It is not only possible, but demonstrably true, that salespeople can market themselves as brands. The wealthiest salespeople do that. In fact, they do it so well that a lot of them eventually stop selling and spend their lives trying to teach others to do what they have done. There is a salesperson in the South who sold windows for a living and made $350,000 per year! He had a 91% close rate! How is that possible? It's actually very straightforward. First, he obviously works very hard. Second, he sets goals. Third, he markets himself as a brand. He sells his company. He sells its product lines. But, he also sells himself.

I run into people like this in my seminars. There are not a lot of them, but there are enough to prove the point that this can be done. It can be done because you don't have to have a national reputation to be successful in sales. You just need to be known within the local market. You can, in fact, be the big fish in a small pond.

Do you remember how exponential growth works? If I want to count to one million, it's going to take me a long time. I have to write down a million numbers. If I count by doubling numbers – 1, 2, 4, 8, 16, 32, etc. – I get there really fast. Actually, I only have to write down 21 numbers before I get to a million.

In selling, if I do a good job for a customer and the customer is satisfied but not particularly 'delighted' with me or my company, I know from research that the customer **will not tell anyone about me**. If I want to find another customer I'll have to get one myself. If I want a hundred customers this year I'll need to go find all 100.

But what if I do a great job? What if the customer is delighted? What if the customer really likes doing business with me? I know from research that **the customer will tell other people about me!** Maybe they'll tell their friends. With some of today's computer aids, like Angie's List, that customer might tell hundreds of other folks.

Now customers start calling me! If a lot of them tell their friends about me, in a short time I have a reputation. I am becoming a 'brand' that people look for. My customer base is starting to grow exponentially.

You only need to be well enough known that people remember your existence when the time is right. "*Oh, you need some work done? Well, you should call this guy that my brother used. He's supposed to be really great. Do you want me to get his number for you?*"

REFERRALS ARE AT THE HEART OF PERSONAL MARKETING.

It's up to you to create a referral network. I've talked about this many times before. Your goal must be to get the order but also to get a customer for life. Every customer might buy again. Every customer certainly knows other people who might buy. They could tell those people about you. So referrals are the way you build your customer base for the future.

There are two ways to get referrals. One is simply to do an outstanding job with every client. The other is to ask.

'Very satisfied' customers tell others.

When you get your car repaired, do you get a survey form from the dealer asking how satisfied you were with the service you received? When you travel, do you get surveyed later by the hotel chain where you stayed? We all get surveyed nowadays. I won't bore you with all the details, but will remind you that this is all an offshoot of the quality process that changed global business beginning in the 1960s and 70s and continues today. The slogan "*At Ford, Quality Is Job One*" isn't just a slogan. It's a critical issue in survival. People no longer tolerate poor quality. They don't have to. There is enough supply out there that if they are not happy with one company, there are many others that they can choose from.

This revolution in quality had an important marketing outcome. Companies discovered that customers whose expectations are exceeded will do two things. First, they'll buy the product again or they'll do business with you again in the future. Second, they'll tell other people about you.

Interestingly, people whose expectations are only 'met,' **may or may not** do business with you again, and **won't tell** others about you. This is not intuitively obvious to many people. A lot of us assume that if the customer is 'satisfied,' then we have done our job. Not so. Customers who are merely satisfied are essentially indicating that doing business with you was 'okay'… just okay.

If you are very satisfied or delighted with your car dealer or your hotel chain or your restaurant, you **will** go back and you **will** recommend them if asked. If you're just satisfied, you **might** not go back, and you won't recommend them. That's why you get surveyed so often. Companies want to know whether they are performing at a level that will earn your business in the future.

This really has critical implications for any in-home salesperson who wants to do business through future referrals. You have to **exceed** your customer's expectations! The T.R.U.S.T.® sales process is designed to do just that, to **exceed expectations**. Customers don't **expect** salespeople to take the time to understand them as individuals; when you use the T.R.U.S.T.® process you'll get referrals.

You get more referrals if you ask.

I bought my last two cars from the same salesperson. His dealership is excellent. The service department is as good as I've seen. I'm 'very satisfied' with them. So I go back.

I've told other people about them, but I've never been asked for a referral. I like the sales guy, but he's never gone out of his way to market himself to me. When I do get a note from him, I can tell it's pre-printed and all he has done is sign it. My impression is business is slow; they decided to send out a mailer; the sales folks just signed them. That's not marketing your personal brand.

This salesperson was in an excellent position to build an ongoing relationship with me, one that would allow him to continuously remind me that 'referrals are always valued and appreciated.'

The most obvious time to ask for a referral is when you close a sale. You can easily build the request into your sales process. Let me give you one example.

Customers like assurance, and they like personal service. You can develop a follow-up process that builds on those customer desires. Make it a point to know when your customer's job is completed. Develop a reason to stop by the customer's home to thank them for their business.

Here are a couple of possible approaches:

- *"I'd like to stop by just to thank you for your business and to give you a small thank you gift if you are going to be around."*
- *"I'd like to stop by and drop off a packet of instruction manuals, warranty cards, and so on."*
- *"I'd like to stop by and be sure you're comfortable with how everything operates."*

This follow-up visit allows you to:

- Thank the customer.
- Leave the customer with several business cards.
- Ask for any referrals, or at a minimum tell the customer directly that you always appreciate referrals.
- Ask the customer directly if they would let you use them as a reference with future customers. If they answer yes, enter them into your references notebook or database.

YOUR PERSONAL MARKETING TOOLS

If you're going to market yourself as a brand, you need some marketing tools. Here are a few suggestions.

Business Cards

Every salesperson should have a business card with a good smiling photo and a personal saying. Write something that fits your business, your customer base, and your personality.

- "*Your personal consultant for comfort and energy savings*"
- "*Making your dreams a reality*"
- "*Expertise you can count on*"
- "*Dedicated to customer satisfaction since 1985*"

Make it easy for people to get in touch with you. Include your business phone number, your cell phone number, and your email address on your card.

Give your business cards out like candy. They are inexpensive, but they get your message out to the customer base.

Personal Mailings

I had a realtor once who contacted me 14 times a year through mailings. Every year he would send out a calendar and a Christmas card. He even hired a mail service to send out a series of postcards every year, each one with a personalized 'I appreciate referrals' message. Every salesperson can find some way to stay in touch with his or her customer base.

For most in-home sellers a once a year mailing is doable. You could consider a holiday greeting with a brief personal message included. It doesn't have to be hand written. You could run off a brief personal message on the computer that would fit most of your clients, but sign it personally. You could develop a brief mini newsletter with some helpful information for your customers coupled with your referral reminder. The important thing is to stay in touch and ask for the referral.

The Checklist

In the preface to this book, I shared my training philosophy with you. I believe that acquiring new skills requires that the learner understand exactly why a skill should be performed in a certain way, understand exactly how that skill is performed, and then have an opportunity to practice that new skill until it becomes the learner's own. Well, I've tried hard to explain to you the why and the how. Now the practice is up to you. To help you along I'm giving you two things. First, I'll give you a list of the 10 specific things that, if you did them on the job, would have the greatest impact on your performance. Second, I've added a final chapter titled 'Staying in Momentum' with some very specific guidance on how to proceed from here. So, here's the list of the top 10 things I would like to see you do. All 10 things are very important, but numbers 1, 2, 3, and 4 will clearly give you the fastest return on your effort.

Tom's Checklist For Sales Success

1. Set key goals and strategies for creating what you want.
2. Treat every customer as an individual.
3. Develop a set of question asking tools.
4. Develop a formal presentation package.
5. Develop a 'choices' proposal.
6. Use an alternate choice finance close.
7. Hone your personal selling skills through regular practice.
8. Focus on referrals.
9. Develop a set of 'personal marketing' tools.
10. Hone your image as a true professional.

All ten of these items have been covered in detail in the preceding chapters, so I hope they all make sense to you. Let me just remind you, though, why each of them is important.

1. Set key goals and strategies for creating what you want.

You don't change outcomes without changing behaviors. **Goals drive change**. If you truly want to do a better job and make more money, then you need to ask yourself, "*To get different results, what things would I need to do differently?*" You'd need to set **goals** and determine **strategies** to do those things. You'd need to **act.** It's that simple. Here's a very realistic suggestion. If you are already in a selling assignment, try setting a goal to increase your annual sales by 25%. I have found that this is a very achievable target for most salespeople. What would you have to do differently to achieve 25% growth? That's your strategy. What tools would you need? Put those down on your calendar and get them done. You can check out the sample goal setting forms included in the appendix.

2. Treat every customer as an individual.

Your job is not to be a product expert, although that's very important. Nor is it your main job to be an expert in job costing, pricing, installation processes, etc. They are all important, too. But all are secondary to your real job. Your number one job is to get **people** to trust you, to share their desires with you, and to want to do business with you and with your company.

This **mindset**, that your job is to influence **people** and not just push **products**, is the primary difference between average and great salespeople. Be a communicator. Be an expert on people.

3. Develop a set of question asking tools.

If you are truly committed to treating people as individuals who are all different from one another, then **questions** become your primary sales tool. "*What do you need?*" "*What do you want?*" "*What constraints do you have?*" We can't know these things unless we **ask**.

I recommend a printed survey form containing both general questions about the customers and their situation, and specific questions designed to bring out the primary benefits you may have to offer the customers.

4. Develop your formal presentation package.

Your presentation materials are your key to looking professional. It also drives your closing process. If you have these tools you will always attempt to close. That's the whole purpose of the presentation, to summarize the customer's needs, to show how your company solves those needs, and to present your proposal.

5. Develop a 'choices' proposal.

Your proposal worksheet should show a choice of solutions. Start with three general packages – best, better and good – and then modify the packages to add specific things that make sense for each specific customer. These would include things such as needed repairs, additions, accessories, and service agreements, etc. This is going to increase your close rate, and it's going to increase your dollars per sale results.

6. Use an alternate choice finance close.

This close is simple, straightforward, and it is a logical extension of your presentation. "*Here are your requirements... here is how our company will meet your requirements... here are two ways to invest in this... which would be better for you?*"

7. Hone your selling skills through regular practice.

If you accomplished item three above, you're going to end up with a much better grasp of questioning skills as a result. There are a number of other basic skills that require your committed practice. The ones covered in this book, benefit selling, objection handling, and closing are particularly critical. Here's what I suggest you do. Take a single skill element and write it down on your calendar. Now **consciously** practice that skill for 30 days. For example, write down "*Use transition phrases.*" Put it right on your calendar where you can see it. Now, as you make each call, you'll be reminded to use phrases like, "*This means that... Let me tell you why this is important... Here's what that does for you...*"

Next month write down a new skill – and practice it. Here are some specific skill elements that I particularly like to see consciously practiced:

- Handling the four most common 'not yet' responses to a closing question.
- Using transition phrases to sell benefits.
- Disarming objections, or any negative feedback.
- Covering multiple benefits for a single feature.
- Asking alternate choice closing questions.

8. Focus on referrals.

Referrals are the lifeblood of top earning salespeople. You get them by doing two things. First, you need to **exceed the expectations** that the customer has for you and for your company. Second, you need to **ask** for the referral.

You exceed your customer's expectations by using the T.R.U.S.T.® selling process. So you need to do that. And you also need to develop strategies for asking for referrals. I discussed some of these strategies earlier in this chapter.

9. Develop a set of 'personal marketing' tools.

Picture yourself as a brand. What kinds of things do you want your brand to express? And what tools would be best to get your brand out in front of the potential customers in your sales area? Get started with something simple… like a creative business card… then add tools as you move forward. I discussed a number of possible tools earlier in this chapter. I think we're getting to a point in technology where every really serious professional in-home salesperson should have a personal website. Think of ways to raise your profile in your local community. Get your picture in the paper. Send postcards to your customer base. Do what it takes to become a local brand.

10. Hone your image as a professional.

I also have talked about the quality process earlier in this book. One of the elements of quality, of continuously exceeding customers' expectations, is the idea of **continuous improvement.** Do you remember in Chapter 1 when I talked about the reason people like selling jobs is because there literally is no 'best?' No matter how good you are, you can be better. You can always find a new skill to learn. You can always become more knowledgeable than you already are. You can always refine you selling tools to make them better. You can always find ways to be a more effective communicator. This is what makes life – and selling – challenging and rewarding. Every year you should be able to look back and say, "*I grew professionally this year.*" Take seminars. Read books. Learn a new product. Upgrade your sales tools. Improve your own personal appearance.

There is nothing that makes me sadder than those occasions when I have an experienced salesperson in one of my seminars who just isn't trying to grasp new ideas because, "*I guess I just always have done it this way.*" That's depressing. Who wants to have a job for 40 years and look back and think, "*Geez that was boring.*"

Life is not what's handed to you. It's what you make out of it. You're in charge. You can fight the system or make it work better for you. You can fight change or you can embrace it. Do you want my advice? Embrace it.

Life is not what's handed to you. It's what you make out of it. You're in charge. You can fight the system or make it work better for you. You can fight change or you can embrace it. Do you want my advice? Embrace it.

CHAPTER 10

Staying In Momentum: What You Need To Do Next Week

In this book I have shared with you enough information and ideas to make you a measurably better salesperson. It doesn't matter how good you are now, how experienced or inexperienced. You can increase your close rate. You can make sure you get more chances than your competitor. You can raise the average value of every sale you make. You can make more money. You can even increase your job satisfaction.

You can do all of this, only if…

I often refer to this Gandhi quotation, "*Be the change you're trying to see in the world.*" Now, Gandhi was literally talking about 'the world,' but the truth in his statement applies just as much to our own daily world as it does to the larger world Gandhi had in mind.

Things will **not** change just because you wish them to or even want them to. You must **be** the change you want to see. You must **act**.

But how? I'm sure you can't remember even a fraction of the hundreds of ideas and strategies you've read in this book. So, I'm going to take these final few pages to tell what, specifically, you would need to do right now to start changing the results you receive and how you can 'Stay in Momentum.'

I sincerely hope that over time you will do a lot of the things I covered in the first nine chapters. I do want you to prepare the best sales tools you can; I do want you to practice the many skills and techniques I covered; I do want you to work on areas like your customer mindset, and think about areas such as customer styles. In order to do any of these things you would probably have to go back and reread a section, make notes, and start to initiate on the job practice. I know it's a huge amount of stuff to bite off… too much, in fact, to do all at once. In this brief chapter I am going to share a technique that will get you started in the right direction, and that will set you up for future development. We're going to start with just one short term, measurable **goal**.

Identify your most important short term performance goal.

Sometime in the next 90 days, I want you to do the **overall** goal setting and strategy development that I talked about in Chapter 9, but for right this moment, let's start simply. What is the most important short term performance goal you want to achieve? Do you want to hit a specific dollar sales goal for this next quarter? Do you want to sell a certain number of jobs? Do you want to achieve a certain close rate? Write down whatever it is that you want to attain.

Determine the actions that would most directly move you toward the goal.

What, specifically, would you need to do to differently right now… tomorrow… to move toward that one goal?

- Would you need to work Saturdays and evenings?
- Would you need to prepare and use a more professional presentation package?
- Would you simply need to change your customer mindset?

- Would you need to develop a financing offering?
- Would you need to be able to improve a certain skill, such as closing on each call?

If you can pick that one goal, and identify just a few needed actions to reach it, you're halfway there.

Now here's how to get all the way there… by being **accountable!**

Be accountable… and ask for help.

Have you… or a friend… ever quit smoking? I was lucky enough not to start, but I had friends who did, and I have seen how hard it is to stop. In my experience, the ones who were able to stop successfully did it by having some **outside** support. They enlisted the aid of a friend or co-worker. They shared their goal with that person, and that person helped them through… reminded them of the goal… badgered them if necessary to keep trying.

I'd like you to do something similar right now. I'd like you to share your most important goal (with its strategies and plans) with another person, and I'd like you to ask them to **hold you accountable** for doing everything you said you'd do. This could be a friend, a business associate, or even your manager if you have the right relationship. This person will ask you what you have done and will not accept excuses. It takes courage, commitment, and resolve to be accountable. When you are, then you can accomplish anything.

Set a formal review date.

Pick a date when you will sit down, alone or with your 'coach,' and formally review your progress. For most people this should be every 30 to 60 days. Keep this as a simple review of your goals, strategies and plans. Focus first on what is working. Congratulate yourself. Now determine what must be changed for those things that are not on track. Identify corrective actions; put them on your calendar; tell your coach what you are going to do.

Repeat... repeat... repeat.

Once you feel that you have made measurable progress toward that one goal, then it will be time to repeat the process. Pick a second goal, or simply move the goal posts out for your first goal. Now, what actions are needed? Write them down. Tell your coach. Make it happen.

> **"Be the change you want to see in the world."**
>
> *- Mahatma Gandhi*

APPENDIX

WHAT YOU SEE:

Furnace
Air Conditioner
Thermostat

WHAT YOU ALSO RECEIVE:

PEACE OF MIND:

- All installers and service technicians wear photo ID
- Special care taken to protect your home during installation
- Drug-free company
- Employees on call 24 / 7
- Preferential service for our Peak Performance customers
- Each job inspected with a 17-point check by installation supervisor

QUALIFICATIONS:

- Experience
- Manufacturers recommendations and local codes are minimum standards
- Licensed, bonded, and insured
- Factory trained installation & service technicians
- Service trucks with genuine factory parts
- Expertise in all home comfort problems

FINANCIALS:

- Comfort guaranteed in writing
- Financial strength
- Multiple finance choices
- 'Heat loss' and 'heat gain' load calculation on every home

Sales Goals and Performance Evaluation

Name:		**Date:**
Year:	**Quarter:**	**Eval. Date:**
Supervisor:		

Annual Goals:	**YTD Goals:**	**YTD Results:**
1.	**1.**	
2.	**2.**	
3.	**3.**	
4.	**4.**	
5.	**5.**	

Key Strategies:	**YTD Results:**
1.	
2.	
3.	
4.	
5.	

Short Term Action Plan:
1.
2.
3.
4.
Comments:

Manager ______________________

Team Member ______________________

Sales Goals and Performance Evaluation

Name: Tom Seller		**Date: Oct. 4, 2009**
Year: 2009	**Quarter: 3rd**	**Eval. Date: Oct. 5, 2009**
Supervisor: John Manager		

Annual Goals:	**YTD Goals:**	**YTD Results:**
1. $1,200,000	1. YTD $800,000	$850,000
2. Close rate 42%	2. 42%	40%
3. 94% of book	3. 94% of book	92% of book
4. RPA $6,000	4. RPA $6,000	RPA $5,850
5. 12% Self Gen	5. 12%	13%

Key Strategies:	**YTD Results:**
1. Use a written Survey form on all calls	Sometimes
2. Use the Presentation Binder on all calls	Never
3. Use Best-Better-Good CHOICES on every call	Using, but not correctly
4. Place yard signs on all sales	Always
5. Hang door hangers 6 x 6 x 6 around all sales	Never

Short Term Action Plan:
1. Use the Survey, Presentation Binder and CHOICES on every call
2. Hang door hangers 6 x 6 x 6 after every sale
3. Always propose a high BEST system
4. Join Le Tip to increase self-gen leads

Comments:
Tom understands that using all of the System Selling tools, placing yard signs and door hangers are not optional and has committed to using them 100% of the time. We will have once-a-week role plays to practice using these tools in October and John will do at least one ride-along in this timeframe for feedback.

Manager ____________________________

Team Member ____________________________

Platinum System Choice	Gold System Choice	Silver System Choice
• Binford Hybrid System • Binford 94% Variable Furnace • Binford 22 SEER 2-Stage 410A A/C • Binford Pureair Filtration • Binford Zoning System • Honeywell Vision Pro 8000 • Whole House Duct Cleaning • Honeywell Co Detector • 1-Year Service Agreement • 10-Year Action Air Warranty	• Binford 94% Variable Furnace • Binford 16 SEER 2-Stage 410A A/C • Binford Healthy Climate Filter • Binford UV Air Treatment • Honeywell Vision Pro 6000 • 1-Year Service Agreement • 5-Year Action Air Warranty	• Binford 80% Variable Furnace • Binford 13 SEER R22 A/C • Binford MERV 10 Air Filter • Honeywell Vision Pro 5000 • 1-Year Service Agreement • Full Factory Warranty
Monthly Investment ____ Total Investment ____	Monthly Investment ____ Total Investment ____	Monthly Investment ____ Total Investment ____

Action Air's Attention to the Details:

- ☐ New outside electrical disconnect
- ☐ New wiring to existing main panel
- ☐ New _____ AMP service
- ☐ New outdoor condensing unit pad
- ☐ Vibration isolation pads
- ☐ New properly sized refrigerant lines
- ☐ Vibration isolation refrigerant lines
- ☐ Exposed lines in protective pipe
- ☐ Insulate refrigeration lines
- ☐ Install refrigerant dryer
- ☐ Charge to manufacturer's specs
- ☐ Replace ___ return air grills
- ☐ Replace ___ supply air registers
- ☐ New condensate pump
- ☐ Condensate to be drained to _______
- ☐ Install emergency condensate drain
- ☐ Provide external combustion air
- ☐ New gas piping
- ☐ New low voltage wiring
- ☐ New insulated return air plenum
- ☐ Install radius turns on ductwork
- ☐ Install internal turning vanes
- ☐ Mastic sealing of installed ductwork
- ☐ Balance air flow throughout system
- ☐ Install manual balancing dampers
- ☐ New double-wall chimney liner
- ☐ All employees certified drug free
- ☐ Installers arrive on time
- ☐ Installers have photo ID
- ☐ Installers courteous and professional
- ☐ Protect the home with drop cloths
- ☐ Wear protective shoe covers
- ☐ Use protective gloves
- ☐ Maintain clean work areas
- ☐ Remove existing equipment
- ☐ Recycle existing equipment
- ☐ Complete system start-up
- ☐ 17-point system Performance Check
- ☐ All legal permits included

Save Money ***Peace Of Mind*** ***Improve Family Health*** ***Quieter Operation***
More Comfort ***More Convenient*** ***Protect Environment*** ***Save Time***

Action Air Design Specialist: ________________________________

COMPANY LOGO

HOME COMFORT, HEALTH AND ENERGY SAVINGS SURVEY

Customer Name(s)____________________ Date of Survey __________

Address____________________ City__________ State _____ Zip __________

Home Phone __________ Work Phone __________ Email__________

1 Family Comfort and Health Preferences

Includes temperature, air movement, air quality, noise level and automatic control convenience.

- How long have you lived here?__________ How long do you plan to live here? __________
- What would you like to see improved in your current system? __________
- What do you like about your current system? __________
- Where in the home does the family spend most of their time? __________ Least? __________

Do you have any of the following problems or concerns? Please rank each as VERY Important or NOT Important to help us show you the best CHOICES:

Problem or Concern	Yes/ No	Comments	Importance
Would you like to reduce indoor / outdoor system noise?			
Uncomfortable temperature swings or drafts?			
Rooms that are too hot or too cold?			
Do you frequently make adjustments to the thermostat?			
Anyone suffer from allergies to airborne dust, mold, pollen, viruses or dander?			
Any other concerns about indoor air quality?			
Is the air too dry in the winter?			
Is there excessive humidity in winter or summer?			
"Stale Air" when the house is closed up for a while?			

<COMPANY LOGO>

Home Comfort, Health and Energy Savings Survey

2 Energy Savings and the Environment

Includes reducing energy use to save annual utility cost and reduce the impact on the environment.

- How much do you spend to heat and cool your home in a year? Heating $ ________ Cooling $ ________
- Have you done any energy savings projects in your home? Describe. ________
- Have you made any additions or changes to your home? ________ Planning any? ________

- How important is saving money on monthly utility bills?
- How important is a *Return on Investment* with a new system?
- Is the "environmental friendliness" of the system an important concern to you?

Very/Not	Comment

3 You and Your Family's Peace of Mind

Includes system reliability, contractor reputation and freedom from repair worries.

- What prompted you to call our company? ☐ Current Customer ☐ Reputation ☐ Referral ☐ Ad in: ________ ☐ Other: ________
- Do you know anyone we have done work for? ☐ Yes ☐ No If yes, please list: ________
- Do you have, or have you ever had, a Maintenance Agreement on your heating and cooling system? ☐ Yes ☐ No If yes, with whom? ________

- How important is owning a comfort system that will last a long time?
- How important is not having to worry about repair bills after the standard warranty is over?
- How important is having a reputable contractor doing work in your home?
- How important is having a contractor you can call 24 hours, 7 days a week?
- How important is getting maintenance reminders?
- Would you like to get our free newsletter with money-saving tips, simple do-it-yourself stories, and customer-only offers? ☐ Yes ☐ No

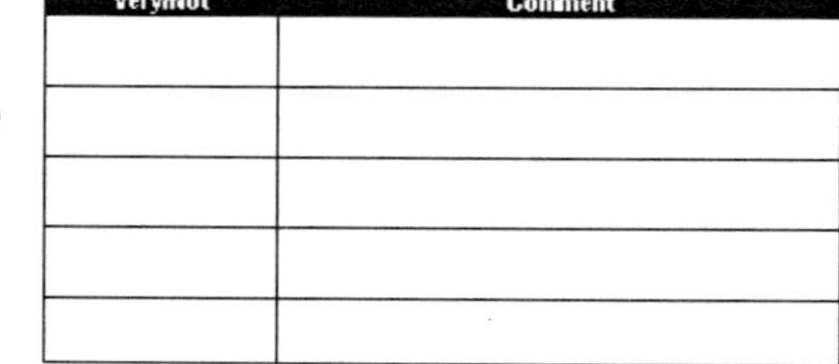

Very/Not	Comment

Now, you can transfer your customer's answers from Parts 1, 2, and 3 to the next page...

<COMPANY LOGO>

HOME COMFORT, HEALTH AND ENERGY SAVINGS SURVEY

Customer's Interests		How Important	Possible HVAC System Solutions
1 **Comfort** • Temperature • Air Movement • Air Quality • Noise Level • Control Convenience	**Quiet** system		☐ Variable fan ☐ Greater Technology ☐ Additional Return Ducting ☐ Insulating Ductwork ☐ Vibration Dampers ☐ Duct Sealing ☐ New Registers ☐ Other________
	Even temperatures throughout the home		☐ Variable Speed Furnace or Air Conditioner ☐ Electronic Thermostat ☐ Zoning Control System ☐ Duct Sealing
	Control **temperature automatically**, day or night		☐ Programmable Electronic Temperature Control ☐ Other________
	Control different areas of the home **independently**		☐ Zoning Control System ☐ Other ________
	Reduce dust, mold, pollen, bacteria & viruses		☐ Electronic Air Cleaner ☐ Media Air Filter ☐ UV Light ☐ Variable Speed Fan ☐ Additional Return Air Ducting ☐ Duct Cleaning ☐ Duct Sealing ☐ Other ________
	Reduce dryness in winter		☐ Whole house humidifier ☐ Other ________
	Reduce **winter moisture**		☐ Air-To-Air Heat Exchanger ☐ Whole House Ventilation Fan ☐ Duct Sealing
	Reduce **summer humidity**		☐ Properly Sizing and Designing A/C ☐ Portable Dehumidifier for Hot Water System ☐ Duct Sealing ☐ Other________
	Add fresh air to the home		☐ Air-To-Air Heat Exchanger ☐ Whole House Ventilation Fan ☐ Other ________
2 **Energy Efficiency** • Savings • Environmental impact	Energy efficient system that **saves money** on utility bills		☐ High Efficiency Furnace ☐ Boilers and Air Conditioners ☐ Variable Speed Fan ☐ Programmable Electronic Thermostat ☐ Electronic Air Cleaner ☐ Media Air Filter ☐ Maintenance Agreement ☐ Duct Sealing ☐ Outdoor Temperature Control
	Energy efficient system helps **protect environment**		☐ High Efficiency Furnaces ☐ Boilers and Air Conditioners ☐ Variable Speed Fan ☐ Air Conditioners with 410A Refrigerant ☐ Other ________
3 **Peace of Mind** • Worry free • Security • Bonuses	A system that will **last as long as possible**		☐ Maintenance Agreement ☐ Top-Of-The-Line Equipment and Accessories
	No worries about repairs		☐ Extended Warranty Included ☐ Maintenance Agreement
	Reputable contractor		☐ Our Company ☐ Testimonials ☐ Confidence ☐ Reliability
	Extended **Service** Hours		☐ Maintenance Agreement ☐ Additional benefits? ________
	Service **Reminders**		☐ Regular contact ☐ Maintenance Agreement
	Customer Newsletter	☐ Yes ☐ No	☐ Greater Company professionalism ☐ More information wanted.

THE BIG PICTURE

MY MINDSET

1. Every customer is a unique individual with different needs / wants.
2. My job is to understand each customer so that I can propose solutions that best fit their needs / wants.
3. When my customers choose me and my company they will get a great value for their investment and be very happy that they chose us.

MY GOAL FOR EACH CALL

1. Gain customer agreement to take action by proposing the best solution for that customer.
2. Achieve a level of customer satisfaction that will cause this customer to call me again in the future and to refer other customers to me.

SELLING WITH T.R.U.S.T.®

T **T**ruth – honesty in all aspects of the sale
R Create a **R**elationship
U **U**nderstand the customer's needs / wants
S **S**how the customer choices
T **T**ake action

THE T.R.U.S.T.® SELLING PROCESS

1. Approach with Discovery
2. Prepare Choices
3. Present
4. Propose
5. Close

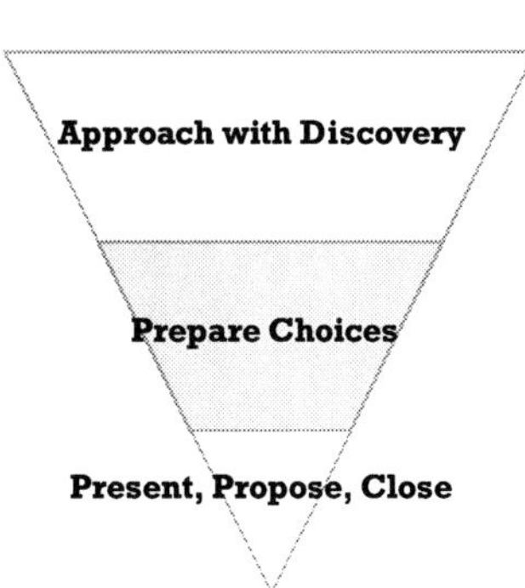

THE 10-STEP T.R.U.S.T.® IN-HOME SALES PROCESS

Approach with Discovery

Step 1 Prepare mentally; have the right mindset.

Step 2 Gather and organize company and supplier material.

Step 3 Check your appearance and focus.

Step 4 Greet the customer and make a strong first impression.

Step 5 Discover the customer's wants and needs, and complete any required physical survey of the job.

Prepare Choices

Step 6 Prepare your proposal.

Present, Propose and Close

Step 7 Present the proposal.

Step 8 Ask for the order and respond to questions or objections.

Step 9 Make the sale and give reassurance.

Step 10 Take 'customer-for-life' actions.

NOTES

NOTES

NOTES

NOTES

NOTES

NOTES

NOTES

NOTES

NOTES

NOTES

Breinigsville, PA USA
16 February 2011
255558BV00004B/1/P

9 780615 320809